The Other Synaesthesia

SUNY SERIES
LITERATURE...IN THEORY

SERIES EDITORS

David E. Johnson, *Comparative Literature, University at Buffalo*
Scott Michaelsen, *English, Michigan State University*

SERIES ADVISORY BOARD

Nahum Dimitri Chandler, *African American Studies, University of California, Irvine*
Rebecca Comay, *Philosophy and Comparative Literature, University of Toronto*
Marc Crépon, *Philosophy, École Normale Supérieure, Paris*
Jonathan Culler, *Comparative Literature, Cornell University*
Johanna Drucker, *Design Media Arts and Information Studies, University of California, Los Angeles*
Christopher Fynsk, *Modern Thought, Aberdeen University*
Rodolphe Gasché, *Comparative Literature, University at Buffalo*
Martin Hägglund, *Comparative Literature, Yale University*
Carol Jacobs, *German and Comparative Literature, Yale University*
Peggy Kamuf, *French and Comparative Literature, University of Southern California*
David Marriott, *History of Consciousness, University of California, Santa Cruz*
Steven Miller, *English, University at Buffalo*
Alberto Moreiras, *Hispanic Studies, Texas A&M University*
Patrick O'Donnell, *English, Michigan State University*
Pablo Oyarzun, *Teoría del Arte, Universidad de Chile*
Scott Cutler Shershow, *English, University of California, Davis*
Henry Sussman, *German and Comparative Literature, Yale University*
Samuel Weber, *Comparative Literature, Northwestern University*
Ewa Ziarek, *Comparative Literature, University at Buffalo*

The Other Synaesthesia

SUSAN BERNSTEIN

Cover Credit: "On White II," by Wassily Kandinsky, 1923. Public domain.

© 2023 State University of New York

All rights reserved

Printed in the United States of America

No part of this book may be used or reproduced in any manner whatsoever without written permission. No part of this book may be stored in a retrieval system or transmitted in any form or by any means including electronic, electrostatic, magnetic tape, mechanical, photocopying, recording, or otherwise without the prior permission in writing of the publisher.

For information, contact State University of New York Press, Albany, NY
www.sunypress.edu

Library of Congress Cataloging-in-Publication Data

Name: Bernstein, Susan, 1957– author.
Title: The other synaesthesia / Susan Bernstein.
Description: Albany, NY : State University of New York Press, [2023] | Series: SUNY series, literature ... in theory | Includes bibliographical references and index.
Identifiers: LCCN 2022046663 | ISBN 9781438493626 (hardcover : alk. paper) | ISBN 9781438493633 (ebook) | ISBN 9781438493619 (pbk. : alk. paper)
Subjects: LCSH: Synesthesia in literature. | Synesthesia—Philosophy. | LCGFT: Literary criticism.
Classification: LCC PN56.S95 B47 2023 | DDC 809—dc23/eng/20230124
LC record available at https://lccn.loc.gov/2022046663

10 9 8 7 6 5 4 3 2 1

In memoriam Werner Hamacher

Contents

Acknowledgments	ix
Introduction: Against Bouba and Kiki	1
Chapter 1 Synaesthesia and Community	9
Chapter 2 Synaesthetic Reading: Liszt's Double Vision	25
Chapter 3 Baudelaire's Synaesthesia	39
Chapter 4 Nietzsche, Wagner, and "Demonic Communicability"	61
Chapter 5 The Unworking of Synaesthesia in Joris-Karl Huysmans's *À Rebours*	73
Chapter 6 Correspond*a*nces: Between Baudelaire and Heidegger	91
A Note on Rhythm	109
Notes	111
Bibliography	123
Index	131

Acknowledgments

This book has long been underway, and I am grateful for the patient support of all of my friends, family, and colleagues at Brown University and beyond who supported its composition. Thanks to the Cogut Institute and the Pembroke Center at Brown University for the opportunity to present parts of the book as work in progress. Parts of chapters 1 and 3 appeared under the title of "The Other Synaesthesia" in *Points of Departure: Samuel Weber between Spectrality and Reading*, edited by Peter Fenves, Kevin McLaughlin, and Marc Redfield, Northwestern University Press, Evanston, IL 2016. A version of chapter 6 appeared in *Modern Language Notes* 130, no. 3 (April 2015); and a French version of chapter 4 was published in *L'énigme Nietzsche*, edited by Isabelle Alfandary and Marc Golschmidt, Editions Manucius, Paris, 2019.

Introduction

Against Bouba and Kiki

Ce qui serait vraiment surprenant, c'est que le son *ne pût pas* suggérer la couleur, que les couleurs *ne pussent pas* donner l'idée d'une mélodie, et que le son et la couleur fussent impropres à traduire des idées.

What would be truly surprising would be if sound *could not* suggest color, if colors *could not* give the idea of a melody, and if sound and color were unsuitable for translating ideas.

—Charles Baudelaire

Synaesthesia (from the Greek, sun- , with, + aesthesis, feeling or perception) today is generally taken to mean a physiological condition that has become the object of interest for experimental psychology and neuroscience. This book contests the suggestion that physiological or neurological synaesthesia is the basis or foundation for the aesthetics of synaesthesia in literature and philosophy that will be examined here. That is, I reject the binary of literal/figurative as mapped onto a body/mind dichotomy that suggests that neurological synaesthesia is the "real" or "true" synaesthesia, of which aesthetic synaesthesia is a mere copy or aftereffect. Richard E. Cytowic and David M. Eagleman, leading scientific scholars of synaesthesia, make a point of distinguishing "genuine" and "pseudo-synaesthesia" by severely limiting the purvey of the term.

> There is confusion about the word "synesthesia" given that it had been used over a 300-year period to describe vastly different things ranging from poetry and metaphor to deliberately contrived

mixed-media applications such as psychedelia, son et lumière, odorama, and even cross-disciplinary educational curricula. Therefore we have to carefully separate those who use synesthesia as an intellectual idea of sensory fusion—artists such as Georgia O'Keeffe, who painted music, or the composer Alexander Scriabin who included light organs in his scores—from individuals with genuine perceptual synesthesia. (13)

We see here the hierarchical division between "genuine," lively sense perception, spontaneity, and what is contrived, that is, unnatural, and intellectually mediated. One is clearly valued over the other.

Cytowic and Eagleman suggest that the neurological connection between or among senses forms the basis of metaphor, which then is understood as a kind of drying up or abstraction from the "natural ground" of the body's physiology. This thinking yields a genealogy of language modeled like this: "perception—synesthesia—metaphor—language" (166).

Cytowic and Eagleman write: "Orderly relationships among the senses imply a cognitive continuum in which perceptual similarities give way to synesthetic equivalences, which in turn become metaphoric identities, which then merge into the abstractions of language. . . . Metaphor is therefore the reverse of what people usually assume. It depends not on some artful ability for abstract language but on our *physical interaction* with a concrete, sensuous world" (166). Even at the "sublinguistic" levels, similarity and equivalence are at work, the perception of which, according to Aristotle, constitutes poetic genius and the ability to make metaphors. Thus the essence of metaphor—likeness—could just as well underpin the possibility of synaesthesia as the reverse.

The perception of likeness—the ability to make metaphor—is a linguistic function. It likewise underlies the famous "bouba" and "kiki" experiment. In this experiment, people are shown images of an amoeba-like blob and a starlike shape and are asked to pair with them the names "bouba" and "kiki." Cytowic and Eagleman write: "98% pick the spiked shape as 'kiki' because its visual jags mimic the 'kiki' sound and the sharp tongue inflection against the palate. By contrast, the blob's rounded *visual* contours are more like the *sound* and *motor* inflections of 'bouba'" (165). Again, similarity and mimicry underlie the very possibility of the association of a linguistic sound and a visual shape; the ability to make metaphor thus could be fully independent of any sort of "innate" or physiological synaesthetic connection between sound and vision. This example is read as a proof of the universality of a sort of proto-synaesthesia. Cytowic and Eagleman explain: "This kind of correspondence across cultures illustrates the rule that pre-existing relationships (analogies) are often co-opted in biology. In this way, synesthetic associations our ancestors established long ago grew into the more abstract expressions we know today—and this is why metaphors make sense" (165–66). They thus endorse a kind of neuro-Cratylism that naturalizes language and privileges nature over culture.[1]

Cytowic and Eagleman refer us to an article called "Synaesthesia—A Window into Perception, Thought and Language" by V. S. Ramachandran and E. M. Hubbard, who provide a bit more detail on some of the issues I have just touched upon.[2] We read that synaesthesia is caused by a "cross-wiring" of different parts of the brain. "We propose," they write, "that synaesthesia is caused by cross-wiring between these two areas, in a manner analogous to the cross-activation of the hand area by the face in amputees with phantom arms" (9). Analogy, or the perception of similarity, is at the very heart of this scientific explanation, which gives rise to the metaphor of "cross-wiring"—a metaphor that perhaps describes "metaphor" itself as a crossing over. This "crossing over" is doubly metaphorized in their explanation of the origin of metaphor in synaesthesia: "It has often been suggested that concepts are represented in brain maps in the same way that percepts (like colours or faces) are. . . . perhaps many [other] concepts are also represented in non-topographic maps in the brain. If so, we can think of metaphors as involving cross-activation of conceptual maps in a manner analogous to cross-activation of perceptual maps in synaesthesia" (17). Again, analogy links the workings of synaesthesia to the metaphor to which it gives rise, and it is perhaps the crossing of metaphor that grounds the possibility of transfer from the senses to sense.

Ramachandran and Hubbard present the bouba and kiki case with a bit more detail and nuance. They describe the reason that so many people attribute the names as predicted as follows: "The reason is that the sharp changes in visual direction of the lines in the right-hand figure [kiki] mimics the sharp phonemic inflections of the sound kiki, as well as the sharp inflection of the tongue on the palate. The bouba/kiki examples provides our first vital clue for understanding the origins of proto-language, for it suggests that there may be natural constraints on the ways in which sounds are mapped on to objects" (19). The connection between name and image is made by *mimicry*, or an originary mimesis, that gives rise to something like an onomatopoeic theory of the origin of language (as they note). This raises the problem of whether there is such a thing as a universal symbolism of language; but the "bouba and kiki effect" only points to an originary imitation, not to a generation, of the shape by the sound, in which case the attributions are originally metaphorical.

The term *synaesthesia* is in fact much older than the three centuries that Cytowic and Eagleman attribute to it. This is indeed the age of the currently defined understanding of it as a neurological condition, of which Kevin T. Dann provides a thorough genealogy and intellectual history in *Bright Colors Falsely Seen: Synaesthesia and the Search for Transcendental Knowledge*. But the term can be found as early as Aristotle, in whose *Nichomachean Ethics* it appears to signify a perception shared among friends in a polity. It develops and is later conflated with the term for a sense that unifies the other senses and points to an emerging concept of self-consciousness. This book addresses the articulation of synaesthesia in a postscientific age, beginning with Baudelaire, but also taking into account later interpretations of Aristotle. The synaesthesia of this book—*The Other Synaesthesia*—is not the neurological condition, but rather the articulation of the connections among the senses and the arts found in literature and philosophy, a sense of synaesthesia that stands on its own. The book does not present a unified theory of synaesthesia, but seeks only to trace its movements and workings in the texts it investigates. This includes the notion of correspondence, which doubles the structure of synaesthesia itself, or marks out its "verticle" dimension: the connection of the senses not only among each other (synaesthesia), but also between the senses (as sensation) and sense (as in signification or meaning), thus as the very meeting place between the body and the mind. Synaesthesia, like metaphor, crosses all of these borders.

For Kevin T. Dann, aesthetic synaesthesia is aimed at discovering a primordial unity or a cosmic synthesis; he describes it as the "ultimate holism—that offering a unified sensory grounding for all human perception" (42). But while synaesthesia holds elements together in a sort of community, the senses and arts never quite fuse, but rather individuate and articulate themselves through their interconnection. In this book, I question the easy dismissal of synaesthesia as a totalizing, idealizing, and "romanticizing" trope and ask whether it cannot also be seen as a power of disarticulation, unworking, and difference. I understand synaesthesia to refer not only to the combination and crossing of the senses but also to the combination and crossing of the arts. While synaesthesia is generally read as a figure of transcendence and unity, there is also another effect of synaesthesia—another feeling of and for the relation of the arts that articulates differences and displaces the position of essence. This other synaesthesia opens up within or alongside of the more familiar sense of synaesthesia as synthesis and points to an alternative understanding of the arts that does not see them as parts of a unified aesthetic whole. This book looks at this language of connection that resists unification to understand the workings of synaesthesia and the interarts in philosophy and literature.

The chapters of this book read the workings and unworkings of synaesthesia in a range of authors to go beyond the usual "There it is!" to examine the function and operations of synaesthesia and correspondence as they are articulated in texts. That is, this book is about discursive formations and not about perception itself. Chapter 1, "Synaesthesia and Community," works with Jean-Luc Nancy's conception of community to open up possible meanings of synaesthesia. This conception articulates a rhythmic "being-with" that first allows the elements it connects to come into being. I trace the verb back to *sunaisthanesthai* in Aristotle through a reading of Giorgio Agamben and his focus on "shared perception" to argue for a rhythmic notion of synaesthesia that connects elements without fusing or unifying them. The chapter pursues the connection between synaesthesia and the relation among the arts to show how the interaction of arts and media resists totalization in Nancy, Adorno, and Benjamin. Adorno and Benjamin also develop the term *constellation* to evoke a similar tension, and I argue that *constellation* and *synaesthesia* are related terms.

Chapter 2, "Synaesthetic Reading: Liszt's Double Vision," considers the open correspondence between Franz Liszt and George Sand. The figure of synaesthesia, as a joining of the senses in the act of reading, models at the same time an experience of quasi-transcendence and the opening of a kind of friendship that connects, but does not unify, its members. Sand compares her experience of Liszt to Lavater's physiognomic reading of heads. The Aeolian harp extends the subject beyond its limits, but does not quite allow it to exceed itself to the point of a genuine transcendence. Correspondence opens not in Swedenborg's mystical synaesthesia, but in the syncopated relation of the senses and the arts in the act of interpretive reading.

In chapter 3: "Baudelaire's Synaesthesia," I consider the canonical foundation of the discourse of synaesthesia and correspondence in poems and prose by Charles Baudelaire. Pointing to the many sources Baudelaire identifies for the theory of correspondence, I suggest that citation and repetition form a kind of community. The figure of synaesthesia joins the senses, while the understanding of art as translation and correspondence joins different artists in a citational community. The community that comes into being in this way is not a group of psychological subjects, but rather is a collection of terms that are held apart even as they are grouped together. What connects them does so alogically, through the materiality of language; it not only connects, but also fragments, serializes, expands, and realigns. The simple stating and exposure of proper names takes up the space through which a sort of community spreads itself. But this type of synaesthesia or community does not gather together presences or aggregate individuals through presence into a whole. Rather, through resonance and dislocation, to use the language of Jean-Luc Nancy, each singular plural—the many singulars—are exposed, set out and brought into play. The chapter takes up a number of poems from *Les Fleurs du Mal* and several of the *Salons*.

Chapter 4, "Nietzsche, Wagner, and 'Demonic Communicability,'" investigates Wagner's notion of the total work of art to show that it develops a type of transcendence contrary to the tense finitude of synaesthesia. The *Gesamtkunstwerk*, for Wagner, implies a logic of incarnation in representation that moves from the poet to the actor to the hero in what Nietzsche, in the *Untimely Meditations*, calls an event of communication ("Mittheilung"). This sympathetic partitioning communication, grounded in Wagner's "demonic communicability," coincides with synaesthesia. Synaesthesia is thus connected with artistic communication as a simultaneous sharing and partitioning that, according to Nietzsche, extends to incorporate the spectator as well. This communicability is inherently reversible; I analyze Nietzsche's turn against Wagner as an effect of this reversibility. The chapter contrasts the later Nietzsche's work, *Der Fall Wagner*, with his earlier celebration of Wagner in "Richard Wagner in Bayreuth."

Chapter 5, "The Unworking of Synaesthesia in Joris-Karl Huysmans's *À Rebours*," reads synaesthesia in this novel against the backdrop of Max Nordau's evaluation of synaesthesia as degenerate. For him, the dissolution of boundaries entails a dissolution of differences and a regression to a less developed stage, equated with the mollusk. Tracing out the alliances of the senses and the arts, the chapter shows how they revolve in a kind of rhythmic interaction that presupposes their differences even in putting them into relation with one another. The chapter focuses first on the ekphrases of Gustave Moreau's paintings of Salomé, and then on Huysmans's analysis of Mallarmé, in particular his dramatic poem "Hérodiade," to show how synaesthesia connects arts and artists without collapsing differences.

Chapter 6, "Correspond*a*nces: Between Baudelaire and Heidegger," considers Heidegger's critique of the correspondence theory of truth in relation to the tradition of *correspondances* established throughout the book. It likewise investigates the concept of *Entsprechung* as correspondence.

Heidegger explicitly translates *Entsprechung* as *correspondance* in his lecture, "What Is philosophy?," originally delivered as a lecture in France. There, *Entsprechung* is meant to present an "other" correspondence that is not correspondence. I want to suggest that the introduction of the term *Entsprechung* cannot help but reintroduce the overtones of correspondence as *homoiosis* that Heidegger wants so much to be done with. But in the process, correspondence comes to differ from itself, reinforcing the irreducible differences among languages in translation: German and French, Greek and Latin. The chapter concludes by taking up Werner Hamacher's reading of the self-differentiation of the term *Entsprechung* in *Für—die Philologie*. Here he shows how language misspeaks or unspeaks (*ent-spricht*) the very thing it co-responds to (*entspricht*); it opens up the otherness to which it stands in an inarticulate relation.

Chapter 1

Synaesthesia and Community

In what are perhaps his most well known works, *La communauté désoeuvrée* (*The Inoperative Community*) and *L'être singulier pluriel* (*Being Singular Plural*), Jean-Luc Nancy presents a reworking of the thought of community that is neither communitarian, nor liberal or Romantic.[1] His notion of community entails the exposure of singularities in an existential process that presupposes neither individuals who are then somehow joined (that is, a model of intersubjectivity), nor a model of language as an instrument of connecting preexistent speakers through a communicated content. Drawing on Heidegger's notion of *Dasein* as *Mit-Sein*, Being-with, Nancy sketches community as a sharing or partitioning (*partage*) of existence. The critique is aimed at the model of community as an organism or an organic totality. That is, community cannot be envisioned as the realization of a philosophy or an essence (hence the term *désœuvrée*, *La communauté désoeuvrée*, hereafter *CD*, 14). Instead, community is marked by an absence and an interruption such that it is never fully present, thus always to come. This community to come surpasses the community envisioned by both humanism and communism, both of which imply a coming-to-presence of self to self, or an immanence of human to human. Nor does his concept of community draw on a prior reality belonging to an earlier historical phase, as often envisioned in what he calls the "romantic" concept of community.

In *The Literary Absolute* (1978), Nancy and Philippe Lacoue-Labarthe analyze and critique the organicism of the Romantic model of collaborative community evident, for example, in the collective project of the Athenaeum. Despite the avant-gardism of the collective project, Jena Romanticism, for them, ultimately falls into the dream of a future presence that would overcome its constitutive fragmentation. For Nancy, the organic model of community culminates in fascism as an "incarnated communion" (*Communauté désouevrée*, 87).

Nancy characterizes community as an ecstatic movement that takes place through the exposure and exposition of singularities that constitute existence as finitude. This implies an extension in space and a necessary co-appearing of multiple singularities. This is the structure that Nancy articulates variously in *Être singulier pluriel*, in which he stresses the precedence of the "*avec*," the co- or the "with," over any singularities it may articulate: "L'*avec* est la condition—singulière plurielle—de la présence en général comme co-présence . . . 'avec' est la pré-position de la position en général, et il fait ainsi sa disposition" (*Être singulier pluriel*, 60–61) ("The 'with' is the [singular plural] condition of presence in general [understood] as copresence . . . 'with' is the pre-position of the position in general; thus, it constitutes its dis-position") (*Being Singular Plural*, 40).

Community is this being in common, or the plurality of being singular, as a shared being. As Nancy describes,

> L'être *en* commun signifie que les êtres singuliers ne sont, ne se présentent, ne paraissent que dans la mesure où ils comparaissent, où ils sont exposés, présentés ou offerts les uns aux autres. Cette comparution ne s'ajoute pas à leur être, mais leur être y vient à l'être. (*CD*, 146)

> Being *in* common means that singular beings are, present themselves, and appear only to the extent that they compear (*comparaissent*), to the extent that they are exposed, presented, or offered to one another. This compearance (*comparution*) is not something added on to their being; rather, their being comes into being in it. (*Inoperative Community*, hereafter *IC*, 58)

Without this plurality, there would be nothing at all. In *La communauté affrontée*, written some twenty-five years later as the preface to an Italian edition of Blanchot's *La communauté inavouable*, Nancy points to the difficult ideological baggage of the word *community*. He explains there how he came to substitute for it various compound terms, such as "être-ensemble," "être-en-commun," and finally "être-avec" (*CA*, 42). "J'ai donc préféré en venir à concentrer le travail autour de l'"avec': presque indiscernable du 'co-' de la communauté, il porte pourtant avec lui un indice plus net de l'écartement au Coeur de la proximité et de l'intimité. L'avec' est sec et neutre: ni communion ni atomization, seulement le partage d'un lieu, tout au plus un contact: un être-ensemble sans assemblage" (*CA*, 43) ("Finally I preferred to concentrate the work around the 'with': almost indiscernable from the 'co-' of the community, still it carries with it a clearer index of the spacing at the heart of proximity and intimacy. The 'with' is dry and neutral: neither communion, nor atomization, just the partitioning/sharing of a place, or even more a contact: a being-together without assemblage") (my translation).

Like Nancy, Italian philosopher Giorgio Agamben also characterizes community as an ecstatic movement that takes place through the exposure and exposition of singularities.[2] Agamben describes community as a borderline experience, an experience of the limit that redefines the spatial model of inside and outside. In *The Coming Community*, Agamben writes: "The *outside* is not another space that resides beyond a determinate space, but rather, it is the passage, the exteriority that gives it access. . . . The threshold is not, in this sense, another thing with respect to the limit; it is, so to speak, the experience of the limit itself, the experience of being-*within* and *outside*. The *ek-stasis* is the gift that singularity gathers from the empty hands of humanity"[3] (68). This experience of ek-stasis, exposure or exposition is always singular: thus as it is in its articulated extension.

In an article titled "Friendship," Agamben traces the notion of community as shared existence to book IX of Aristotle's *Nichomachean Ethics*, toward the end of the discussion of friendship in books VIII and IX. Sara Brill has expanded on this idea at length in her recent book, *Aristotle on the Concept of Shared Life*, in which she locates concurrent or shared perception (*sunaisthesis*), as a crucial component of (*suzen*) or shared life. I quote here part of the passage at stake as quoted by Agamben.

> And if, as the good person is to himself, so he is to his friend (since the friend is another self [*heteros autos*], then just as for each his own existence (*to auton einai*) is desirable, so his friends' is too, or to a similar degree. But as we saw, the good man's existence is desirable because of his perceiving [*aisthanesthai*] himself, that self being good; and such perceiving is pleasant in itself. In that case, he needs to be concurrently perceiving [*synaisthanesthai*] his friend—that he exists, too—and this will come about in their living together, conversing and sharing (*koinonein*) their talk and thoughts; for this is what would seem to be meant by "living together" [*suzen*] where human beings are concerned, not feeding in the same location as with grazing animals.[4] (Rowe, as quoted in Agamben, 5)

The blurring or sharing of selves in friendship grounds the being singular plural of community. Synaesthesia is thus fundamental to community as a shared subjectivity that is irreducible to neither self (Brill, 74). "If we take Aristotle's complete argument into account," writes Brill, "however, we must acknowledge that it is not only a matter of perceiving myself when perceiving my friend, or of perceiving my friend as myself, but of perceiving together and knowing together, of *sunaisthanesthai* and *suggnorizein*. And, as Aryeh Kosman put it, 'being conscious together does not indicate being conscious, as it were, side by side, but forming together a partnership of consciousness, a community characterized by the common perception that is *sunaisthesis*'" (Brill, 62).

Following up on Nancy's work and on his own previous work on the *Coming Community*, Agamben specifies: "Friendship is the instance of this concurrent perception of the friend's existence in the awareness of one's own existence. But this means that friendship also has an ontological and, at the same time, a political dimension. The perception of existing is, in fact, always already divided up and shared or con-divided. Friendship names this sharing or con-division" (6).

Community, the political and being singular plural all articulate the relationship of synaesthesia. Synaesthesia would thus name not a unified coperception, but an irreducible space of differentiation connected to the sense of community in Aristotle's *Nichomachean Ethics*. While most literature tends to locate the beginning of interest in synaesthesia, and the coining of the term, in the European seventeenth or eighteenth-century, philological investigation lets us see the ancient Greek connection between community and synaesthesia—a connection that will later be solidified in Wagner's theory of the *Gesamtkunstwerk*. Daniel Heller-Roazen draws attention to the philological history of synaesthesia in his book *The Inner Touch: Archaeology of a Sensation*.[5] From this sense of synaesthesia as a "feeling in common" (81), Heller-Roazen traces the development of synaesthesia to mean the "sense of sensing" that will be attributed to it by Aristotle's interpreters. He shows persuasively how the interpretive tradition came to use the term *synaesthesia* to mean a "self-awareness" or "with-sensation" that underlies all sensing, a kind of precursor to self-consciousness—understood, however, as a self-consciousness without a self. What we would call self would be better indicated by a kind of syncopated self-relation: Heller-Roazen writes: "a structural 'perceiving-with,' by which the perception of perceptual qualities would be, at every moment, necessarily 'joined' to another perception, with which it did not altogether coincide. This would be the natural accompaniment to the execution of every act of sensation. Constantly with it, without being completely one with it, it would tap out the measures, so to speak, of the time in which something was sensed at all" (84). Synaesthesia later becomes identified with the common sense, *koine aisthesis*, understood as the unity that holds together all the senses. According to Priscian (sixth century AD), Heller-Roazen writes, "The central sense is that power in the soul which 'jointly perceives itself' (*heautes sunaesthesetai*), not as a 'self' but as a faculty in which the multiple activities of the senses, all felt at once, reach their 'indivisible unity'" (88).[6]

But before this unification, which will come up again at various times in the tradition of synaesthesia, synaesthesia connects differences without overcoming them, just as the "shared perception" of existence maintains the difference between friends at the same time that it connects them. Take for instance this case described by Wassily Kandinsky in his famous *Concerning the Spiritual in Art*: "A Dresden doctor relates of one of his patients, whom he designates as an 'exceptionally sensitive person,' that he could not eat a certain sauce without tasting 'blue,' i.e. without experiencing a feeling of seeing a blue color" (24). The taste of the sauce and the vision of blue remain distinct, even as they are conjoined. If the difference between them were obliterated, it would not even be possible to identify synaesthesia. This relationship—of a kind of community of the senses—is paralleled in the relation among the arts. Despite their concurrence to a common spiritual goal, writes Kandinsky, the arts remain separate: "And so at different points along the road are the different arts, saying what they are best able to say, and in the language which is peculiarly their own. Despite, or perhaps thanks to, the differences between them, there has never been a time when the arts approached each other more nearly than they do today, in this later phase of spiritual development" (19). The relationship among the arts exerts a resistance to the unification of synaesthesia as a transcendent ideal. As Jean-Luc Nancy points out in "Why Are There Several Arts and Not Just One?" ("Pourquoi y a-t-il plusieurs arts, et non pas un seul? [Entretien sur la pluralité des mondes])," the opening essay in his book *Les Muses, The Muses*, the question of the unity of the arts reaches its high point with the aesthetics of Hegel. Hegel partitions the arts in terms of the senses, though he excludes smell, taste, and touch from the realm of art.[7] The differences among the arts relate to the resistance of materiality to the generalizing tendency of art as the realization of the Idea—Art or the Idea of Art, its unity, is thus the origin and support of the arts in their diversity (cf. Nancy, 23–24). Hegel's notion of the unity of art depends on the sublatability of materiality, that is, of difference; at the same time, his model states the essential exteriority of art, its nature as an extended articulation. Despite the fact that art has its tendency in its own sublation in thought, Nancy writes, "the moment of separate exteriority is nevertheless essential to the very essence of art" (9) ("il n'en reste pas moins que le moment de l'extériorité séparée est éssentiel à l'essence même de l'art") (24).[8]

Nancy will reverse Hegel and take this essential exteriority as his point of departure. He shows first that there is no direct correspondence between the senses and the arts. Touch, for example, which Nancy identifies as the paradigm or even the essence of sense in general, has no corresponding art (27). Nancy further argues for the dissociation of the senses from the arts precisely through the model of Baudelaire's *correspondances*. "Ordinary synaesthesia"—the fusing of the senses—takes place according to the phenomenological model of Merleau-Ponty as "perceptive integration."[9]

> But one quickly realizes that perceptive integration and its lived experience would be more correctly located at the opposite extreme from artistic experience and that poetic "correspondences" do not belong to the register of perceptive unity, which has no knowledge of "correspondence" as such and knows only integrated simultaneity. (Nancy, 12)

> Mais on s'apercoit vite que l'intégration perceptive et son expérience vecue se situaeraient plutôt aus antipodes de l'expérience artistique et que les "correspondances" poétiques ne sont pas du registre de l'unité perceptive, qui ignore la "correspondance" comme telle et ne connaît qu'une simultanéité intégrée. (Nancy, 28)

Ordinary perception thus would always entail a sort of synaesthesia or gathering of the senses, but such that this experience would not be the model that art as synaesthesia could copy. "One can only envision a different synesthesia in nature, *another* sensuous integration, a proper sense of art (or of the senses in art)" (13) ("On peut seulement viser une synesthésie differente en nature, un *autre* intégration sensible, un sens propre de l'art [ou des sens dans l'art]") (29). What might this "other synaesthesia" be? How might it be understood? The principle of this other synaesthesia would be touch, the sense, as Nancy writes, that focuses on an original heterogeneity: "Touch is nothing other than the touch or stroke of sense altogether and of all the senses. It is their sensuality as such, felt and feeling" (17) ("Le toucher n'est autre chose que la touche du sens tout entier, et de tous les sens. Il est leur sensualité comme telle, sentie et sentante") (35). Touch is an original self-differentiation, a syncopated and thus interrupted, non-self-consistent, unity. Rather than overcoming difference, synaesthesia would instead articulate it. The arts articulate. Nancy writes,

> L'indifférence ou la synergie synesthésique ne consistent pas en autre chose que dans l'auto-hétérologie du toucher. La touche des sens pourra donc etre distribuée et classée d'autant de manières que l'on voudra: ce qui la fait être la touche qu'elle est, c'est une dis-location, une hétérogénéisation de principe. (36)

> Indifference or synesthetic synergy consists in nothing other than the auto-heterology of touch. The touch or stroke of the sense may thus be distributed and classified in as many ways as one likes: what makes it into the touch that it is is a dis-location, a heterogeneity in principle. (17–18)

The other synaesthesia interrupts ordinary synaesthesia or normal sense integration (44). To develop this, Nancy turns to Baudelaire's lines. Consider the second stanza of Baudelaire's poem "Correspondances."

> Comme de longs échos que de loin se confondent
> Dans une ténébreuse et profonde unité
> Vaste comme la nuit et comme la clarté
> Les parfums, les couleurs et les sons se répondent. (*OC*, 1, 11)

> Like long echoes from far away, merging into a deep dark unity, vast as night, vast as the light, smells and colors and sounds concur. (Waldrop, 14)

For Nancy, this "se répondre" opens a different kind of relationship, which is neither that of signification nor of sensation but is nevertheless one of communication (45), or we might say of a kind of community (45). Rather than see a fused unity, Nancy refers us to the etymological sense of *re-spondere*, which comes from the Latin verb *spondere*, to give/contract in marriage, or to promise, give a pledge (source of the word *spouse*, from Greek *spendo*, to pour or make a drink offering, a libation).

> La synesthésie dis-loquée, proprement et techniquement *analysée*, engage aussi bien, non pas une autre synthèse, mais un renvoi ou, selon let mot de Baudelaire, une *réponse* de touche à touche qui n'est ni un rapport d'homologie externe, ni une osmose interne, mais ce qu'on pourrait décrire selond l'étymologie de *re-spondere* comme un engagement, une promesse donnée en réponse à une demande, à un appel: les touchers se promettent la communication de leurs interruptions, chacun fait toucher à la différence de l'autre (d'un autre ou de plusieurs autres, et virtuellement de touch, mais d'une totalité sans totalisation). Cette "co-respondance" elle aussi se dégage de la signification. (*Les Muses*, 45)

> The dis-located synesthesia, properly and technically *analyzed*, sets off as well, not another synthesis, but a reference, or, in Baudelaire's terms, a response from one touch to another. This response is neither a relation of external homology nor an internal osmosis, but what might be described, with the etymology of re-spondere, as a pledge, a promise given in response to a demand, to an appeal: the different touchings promise each other the communication of their interruptions; each brings about a touch on the difference of the other (of an other or several others, and virtually of all others, but of a totality without totalization). This "co-respondence" disengages itself from signification. (23)

Baudelaire's correspondence can be read not as a transcendent unity, but as an articulation across space of plurality that promises convergence but does not supply it.

Synaesthesia is not a concept, an interiority that would divide itself into an exterior (a concept), but rather is the pulsing movement of the exterior itself. In this syncopation, the literal sense of touch is dislocated and touches on meaning instead: that is, it shifts from physical touching to touching on, being about, and coming into contact with in a way that is not exclusively physical. In touch, sensation touches itself and touches on sense (36). This is what Nancy calls "*transimmanence.*" Nancy plays on the multiple senses of touch as not only the sensation, but also the meaning of "to speak of," or "to thematize," "to be about"—to touch on.[10]

The shifting between the senses of touch, from senses to sense, parallels the move in Baudelaire from synaesthesia to correspondence. One could say that synaesthesia is the horizontal relation among the senses while correspondence is the vertical relationship of harmony that allows a fundamental tone to resound in its overtones, for example. In an essay on Baudelaire's "Correspondances," Jonathan Culler defines the vertical dimension of the so-called doctrine of correspondence as follows: "The first quatrain, in particular, is seen as echoing a romantic topos: the visible forms of the universe are signs of an invisible spiritual reality. This is the idea of vertical correspondence: relations between material signifiers and spiritual signifieds (or what Baudelaire calls 'cet admirable, cet immortel instinct du beau qui nous fait considéré la terre et ses spectacles comme un aperçu, comme une correspondance du ciel")[11] In Nancy's model, synaesthesia itself articulates the relation of correspondence, that is, there is no correspondence without the interaction of the senses in synaesthesia, no interior to which the exterior would correspond. This preponderance of the exterior is what qualifies the area of art. He writes: "In one way or another, art would thus be in default or in excess of its own concept. . . . Art and the arts interbelong to each other in a tense, extended mode in exteriority, without any resolution in interiority" (*The Muses*, 4) ("art serait donc en défaut ou en excès de son propre concept. . . . L'art et les arts s'entr'appartiennent sans résolution en intériorité, sur un mode tendu, étendu, en extériorité") (*Les Muses*, 16). The dislocation of touch opens up the other synaesthesia within synaesthesia.

Synaesthesia is thus governed by the pulsing of rhythm, but rhythm conceived of only as an articulating force and not as what is articulated. It is what prevents the sublation of the senses into a total work of art. In his essay, "Art and the Arts," Theodor W. Adorno considers the tension between the singular of art and the multiplicity of the arts. According to Adorno, art exists only in the arts (426). On the one hand, "art" stands as a unifying goal while the plurality of the arts remains embedded within the inessential realm of the empirical.

> Trotzdem hat der Begriff der Kunst sein Wahres. . . . Gegenüber den Künsten ist Kunst ein sich Bildendes, in jeder einzelnen insoweit potentiell enthalten, wie eine jede streben muss, und der Zufälligkeit ihrer quasi naturalen Momente durch diese hindurch sich zu befreien.[12]

Notwithstanding this, the concept of art has its truth. . . . In contrast to the arts, art is in the process of formation, it is

> potentially contained in each art form, just as each must strive to liberate itself from the chance nature of its quasi-natural aspects. ("Art and the Arts," *Can One Live after Auschwitz?*, 383)

What the arts have in common is their tendency to dissociate themselves from empirical materiality, a materiality that nevertheless remains essential to them. The utopian element of the arts, that element in them that strives to transcend the real, is in tension with their fundamental inextricability from reality.

> Alle brauchen Elemente aus der empirischen Realität. . . . von der sie sich entfernen; und ihre Realisierungen fallen doch auch in die Empirie. Das bedingt die Doppelstellung der Kunst zu ihrer Gattungen. Ihrem unauslöschlichen Anteil an der Empirie gemäss existiert Kunst nur in den Künsten. . . . Als Antithesis zur Empirie dagegen ist die Kunst eines. (426)

> All require elements taken from the empirical reality from which they distance themselves, yet their products are part of that reality. It is this that conditions the dual stance of art toward its forms. In tune with their inextinguishable involvement in empirical reality, art exists only in the arts. . . . As the antithesis to reality, in contrast, art is one. (383)

Adorno's delineation of the relation among the arts, as all tending toward the singularity of art, resembles Benjamin's description of the relation among languages within the problematic of translation. Benjamin writes that the multiple languages are differentiated in their way of meaning, the "Art des Meinens," while converging around a common things that is meant (*GS*, IV, 1: 14). Adorno maps this same pattern onto the relationship between multiple arts.

> Das Gleiche," writes Adorno, "das die Künste als ihr Was meinen, wird dadruch, *wie* sie es meinen, zu einem Anderen. Ihr Gehalt ist das Verhältnis des Was und des Wie. Kunst werden sie kraft ihres Gehalts. (420)

> The different arts may aim at the same subject, but they become different because of the *manner* in which they mean it. Their

substantial content lies in the relation between the *what* and the *how*. They become art by virtue of this substantial content. (377)

Adorno echoes Benjamin's language of constellation in the following formulation: "The constellation of art and the arts dwells within art itself" (383) ("Die Konstellation von Kunst and Künsten wohnt der Kunst selbst inne") (426). Because artworks get their quality as artworks not only from their producer but also from their materiality, their extended quality remains essential and resists absorption into a conceptual unity.

> Das bringt ein Moment des Irreduziblen, qualitative Vielfältigen ins Spiel. Es opponiert jeglichem Prinzip von Einheit, auch den der Kunstgattungen, kraft dessen, was sie ausdrücken. (418)

> This introduces an element of irreducible, qualitative plurality. It is incompatible with every principle of unity, even that of the genres of art, by virtue of what they express. (375)

In Benjamin's language, art would be an "idea," not a concept; thus the arts would form a constellation whose unity depends on the intensity of the extremes, of the individual work or the singular instance. Benjamin famously defines ideas as follows in his book on the *Origin of German Tragic Drama*:

> Die Ideen sind ewige Konstellationen und indem die Elemente als Punkte in derartigen Konstellationen erfasst werden, sind die Phänomene aufgeteilt und gerettet zugleich. Und zwar liegen jene Elemente . . . in den Extremen zum genauesten zutage. Als Gestaltung des Zusammenhanges, in dem das Einmalig-Extreme mit seinesgleichen steht, ist die Idee umschrieben. (215)

> Ideas are timeless constellations, and by virtue of the elements' being seen as points in such constellations, phenomena are subdivided and at the same time redeemed; so that those elements . . . are most clearly evident at the extremes. The idea is best explained as the representation of the context within which the unique and extreme stands alongside its counterpart. (34–35)

Synaesthesia indicates the gathering of works and arts around an empty center: art or genre, the unity it intends but does not attain. This structure models purposiveness without purpose: an apperception devoid of a concept of what kind of a thing it is supposed to be. Synaesthesia might also be understood to overlap with Benjamin's term, *constellation*, a similarly resistant spatial model.[13] Like synaesthesia, constellation connects without unifying.

Constellation might be understood as a visual and spatial counterpart to the term *resonance*, which similarly stresses difference and distance among the elements it connects. Adhering always to the resounding body ("corps sonore"), resonance implies a historically and materially bound manner of meaning and interpretation. At the same time, resonance maintains a connection to the Pythagorean and neo-Platonic heritage that hears in resonance the harmony of the spheres: that is, a system of mathematical ratios that connects everything in a divinely established order in which everything corresponds to everything else. This worldview finds an echo in the mysticism of Immanuel Swedenborg and its overtones in eighteenth- and nineteenth-century literature. It extends too to recent theorizing about intermediality, which sometimes falls into a naive world of correspondences among the media and the senses, and to eco-poetics, which sometimes poses an unproblematic and seamless passage between "natural" and linguistic forms (Fibonacci sequence, for example).

Adorno draws constellation into his own idiom in comparing it to composition. Composition lays out and extends, creating a context of relation. In this spreading out—comparable to Benjamin's "Abschreitung"—subjectivity reverses into objectivity. "Der Zusammenhang, den sie [die Komposition] stiftet—eben die 'Konstellation'—, wird lesbar als Zeichen der Objektivität: des geistigen Gehalts. Das Schriftähnliche solcher Konstellationen ist der Umschlag des subjektiv Gedachten und Zusammengebrachten in Objektivität vermöge der Sprache" (167–68) ("The subjectively created context—the 'constellation'—becomes readable as sign of an objectivity: of the spiritual substance. What resembles writing in such constellations is the conversion into objectivity, by way of language, of what has been subjectively thought and assembled") (*ND*, 165). Composition and constellation offer a scriptural space in which subjectivity and objectivity interpenetrate one another without sublation. Adorno consistently uses this formulation: "Aber Wahrheit, die Konstellation von Subjekt und Objekt, in der beide sich durchdringen" (133) ("But truth, the constellation of subject and object in which both penetrate each other") (*ND*, 127).

Composition and constellation resemble synaesthesia in bringing points into relation without unifying or sublating them. Synaesthesia is the extended medium of rhythm, a rhythm Nancy defines against Deleuze as one written with a small *r*.¹⁴ It sets up a relation among the arts or the senses that is not continuous with the "ordinary synaesthesia" of Merleau-Ponty, that is, of sensation or sense perception. Nancy writes,

> Le rythme n' 'apparaît' pas, il est le battement de l'apparaître en tant qui celui-ci consiste simultanément et indissociablement dans le movement de venir et de partir des forms of des présences en générale, et dans l'hétérogénéité que espace la pluralité sensitive et sensuelle. (46)

> Rhythm does not *appear*; it is the beat of appearing insofar as appearing consists simultaneously and indissociably in the movement of coming and going of forms or presence in general, and in the heterogeneity that spaces out sensitive or sensuous plurality. (*The Muses*, 24)

The gap of rhythm is opened within and between synaesthesias. In an essay called "On Some Relations between Music and Painting" ("Über einigen Relationen zwischen Musik und Malerei"), Adorno discusses the relation between the two arts as one of convergence, a bending or inclining together, which he will distinguish from the "bad" relationship of Romantic synaesthesia. The two media converge, Adorno writes, in their common quality as writing, "*Schrift*." The difference within writing parallels the gap or rift of synaesthetic rhythm. While this notion of *Schrift* is connected to the *Sprachcharakter* or language-character of the two media, this character is not that of narrating or directly communicative language. Adorno writes,

> Die Konvergenz der Medien wird offenbar durchs Hervortreten ihres Sprachcharakters. Das ist aber das Gegenteil von Sprachgestik, sprechendem Verhalten; von Music oder Malerei, wofern sie etwas erzählen wollen. Sie sprechen durch ihre Beschaffenheit, nicht dadurch, dass sie sich vortragen; sie sprechen um so deutlicher, je tiefer sie in sich selbst durchgebildet sind, und die Figuren ihres Durchgebildetseins sind ihre Schrift.¹⁵

> The convergence of the media is disclosed through the stepping forth of their character as writing [*Schrift*]. But that is the opposite of a language gesture, of a speaking comportment; of music or painting insofar as they want to narrate something. They speak

> through their qualities, not through discursive presentation; they speak all the more clearly the more deeply they are worked through in themselves, and the figures of their being worked through are their script/writing. (My translation)

The character of the two media as writing is defined as its quality as a sign, as a mark different from what it demarcates (as trace).

> Zeichen wird es vermöge eines Bruches zwischen ihm und allem Bezeichneten. Écriture in Musik und Malerei kann keine direkte Schrift sein, sondern nur eine chiffrierte; sonst bleibt es bei der Nachahmung. (634)

> It becomes a sign by virtue of a break between it and any signified. Écriture in music and painting cannot be a direct script, but only an encoded one; otherwise it would stop at imitation.

The convergence of the arts takes place not through imitation or similarity, but through a common event of differentiation, of a break, held fast in the French term *écriture*. This break converges with Adorno's notion of expression which, he is careful to argue, does not imply an expressive or expressing subject. As time articulates itself in painting and space in music—the convergence of the two arts, which I associate with synaesthesia—they show "an affinity with pure expression." They show

> Affinität zum reinen Ausdruck; unabhängig von der signifikativen Beziehung auf ein Auszudrückendes nicht nur, sondern auch von der damit verschwisterten eines sich ausdrückenden, mit sich identischen Subjekts. (635)

> affinity to the pure expression; independent not only of a signifying relationship to something to be expressed, but also from any related thing that would express itself, a subject identical with itself.

Adorno continues: "This affinity is disclosed as a break between sign and signified" ("Diese Affinität wird offenbar als Bruch zwischen Zeichen und Bezeichnetem") (635).

The relation among the arts, or synaesthesia, would not be the simple fusion and unity of the senses, but rather would be a striated, rhythmically interrupted and differentiated network that has to do with its status as writing or script. "Im Reflex darauf (bei Katastrophen) zucken die Künste zusammen; die Spuren solcher Zuckungen, welche die Werke bewahren, sind die Schriftzüge an ihnen" (635) ("In reflex [to catastrophes], the arts move convulsively together; the traces of such convulsions, which the works preserve, are the traits of script in it").

The intermedial games, *Spielereien*, of the early twentieth century (in symbolism and futurism, etc.) for Adorno are strictly to be differentiated from the "immanent convergence" between music and painting that he outlines. This convergence might be characterized by Nancy's term *transimmanence*: a concurrent transcendence which is not one, a movement towards a center or meaning that falls back again on the multiplicities of its articulations rather than heading toward its goal. Adorno explains "bad" synaesthesia—which he calls the synaesthesia of Tristan and Baudelaire—as the horizontal relations among phenomena rather than this verticle convergence toward, rather than as the break or gap within phenomenality itself. Such a regime—bad synaesthesia—heralds repetition and tautology, always negative terms for Adorno.

> Wer sie als Prinzip aufrichtet, möchte zweimal, durch Verkoppelung verschiedener Medien und Ausbeutung übrigens fragwürdiger Analoga einiger ihrer Phänomene, sagen, was einmal bereits gesagt ward. . . . Die Konvergenz von Musik und Malerei ist das Gegenteil solcher Tautologie. Sie vollzieht sich im Sagen selbst, nicht im Gesagten. (637)

> Whoever holds it up as a principle, through the linking of different media and the exploitation of questionable analogies of some of their phenomena, would like to say twice that which has already been said once. . . . The convergence of music and painting is the opposite of this kind of tautology. It is accomplished in the saying itself, not in what is said.

This saying itself—as rhythm that does not land anywhere—is the realm of synaesthesia, of an irreducible plurality linked together but not fused. The community of the arts articulates this rhythmic coperception.

Chapter 2

Synaesthetic Reading

Liszt's Double Vision

In the following passage in his *Letters from Italy*, Percy Bysshe Shelley describes his impression of Raphael's painting of St. Cecilia, the patron saint of music. The passage brings together the questions of transcendence and inspiration. Shelley writes,

> I have seen a quantity of things here—churches, palaces, statues, fountains and pictures; and my brain is at this moment like the portfolio of an architect, or a print-shop, or a common place book. . . . We saw besides one picture of Raphael; St. Cecilia; this is another and higher style; you forget that it is a picture as you look at it; and yet it is most unlike any of those things which we call reality. It is of the inspired and ideal kind. . . . The central figure, St. Cecilia, seems rapt in such inspiration as produced her image in the painter's mind.

Shelley contrasts here two types of vision. One is a slightly prosaic kind that reproduces in his mind various aesthetic images: churches, palaces, statues, fountains, and pictures. He likens his mind, in this kind of vision, to common visual reproductions, like plates in a book. The second type of vision, in contrast, entails a complete forgetting or erasure of the materiality of the painting and moves instead toward an idealized spiritualization or animation of the figure presented there, that is, St. Cecilia. The figure of the saint, herself on the verge of transcendence, is "rapt in inspiration," an inspiration doubling that of the painter himself. Painting, music, and writing come together here to create a scenario in which the spirit of music causes the figure to come alive and transcend her earthly bounds. In Raphael's painting, heaven opens up above the saint while musical instruments lay scattered on the ground. One forgets or leaves behind the material means of the production of music and focuses only on the destined effect, the space of transcendence above the earth. The figure is both inspired and inspiring.

For the Romantic artist, inspiration is qualified by this strange duplicity. We can follow it through even more dramatically in some passages from Franz Liszt's *Lettres d'un bachelier ès musique* (*Letters of a bachelor of music*), a series of open letters published in Parisian musical journals between 1835 and 1841. In his letter to Lambert Massart from Milan, published in the *Gazette musicale* in 1838, Liszt describes the transport he experiences when hearing music at a big party. He writes,

> The music had produced its usual effect on me; it had isolated me in the midst of a crowd; it had wrenched me from the external world only to plunge me into the depths of an interior one. . . . I felt so out of place, so dejected . . . that I left the ballroom in search of a secluded, unoccupied corner where I could be alone. . . . I entered an isolated boudoir. It was furnished in Gothic style and dimly lit by an alabaster lamp that shed its rays on dark clusters of tropical plants. . . . I sat down in a huge armchair whose black carvings and Gothic forms carried my imagination to a past age, while the scent of the exotic flowers conjured up visions of distant climes.[1]

This scenario gives rise to a peculiar dream sequence in which Liszt sees the mysterious figure of a man. The letter continues: "A magnetic force drew me after him. . . . The farther I went, the more it seemed to me that my existence was linked to his, that his breath animated my life, that he held the secret of my destiny, and the we, he and I, had to merge with and transform each other" (95). In this musical transport, Liszt comes into contact with a vision of himself, of himself as inspiration, as an other, an alter ego with whom he cannot quite catch up. "'Oh, whoever you are,' I cried, 'incomprehensible being who has fascinated and taken complete possession of me, tell me, tell me, who are you? Where do you come from? Where are you going? What is the reason for your journey? What are you seeking? Where do you rest? . . . Are you a condemned man under an irrevocable sentence? Are you a pilgrim filled with hope eagerly traveling to a peaceful, holy place?'" (96). This mirror-like figure takes the shape of an Aeolian harp, his tones reaching far beyond that of articulate speech with which it intermittently resounds.

> I noticed that he was holding an oddly shaped musical instrument whose bright, metallic finish shone like a mirror in the rays of the setting sun. An evening breeze rose, carrying with it the notes of the mysterious lyre: broken notes, unconnected chords, vague and indefinite sounds, suggesting at times the crashing of waves over a reef, the murmur of pines defying a tempest, or the confused buzzing of a beehive or large crowds of people. From time to time the music would stop and I heard the following clear words: "Do not trouble to follow me; the hope you attach to my steps is deceptive. Do not ask me what I do not know; the mystery you want to fathom has not been revealed to me." (96)

The stranger's inability to answer Liszt's questions suggests that he really is Liszt himself, with the same lack of knowledge, the same intermittent musical breeze, the same vagueness and indefiniteness of his prose. The figure cannot answer Liszt's questions because he is Liszt himself. In an earlier letter to George Sand, Liszt uses very similar language to describe some of his early compositions: "About that time I wrote a number of pieces that inevitably reflected the kind of fever that was consuming me. The public found them strange and incomprehensible, and even you, my friend [George Sand], have criticized me at times for being vague and diffuse" (18). Music intermittently interrupts the discord of the stranger's being: "At times the breeze coming over the water carries ineffable harmonies to me; I listen to them rapturously, but as soon as I think they are coming nearer, they are smothered by the discordant din of human strife" (97).

The ability to transcend finitude through musical transport is thus only temporary, rising above the waters or emitted from the strange frame of an Aeolian harp in alternation with the facts of reality. This duality is already doubled in Liszt's relation to this image or vision of himself, as an irreducible other whose being is somehow shared with Liszt. This vision of Liszt, or Liszt's vision, is originally split and doubled; Liszt presents a kind of being in the world that ecstatically extends to irreducible relationships with alterity.

Synaesthesia here is not about Swedenborg's theory of correspondence and the way in which it attunes artists and media to one another. Instead, I look at some passages in Liszt's correspondence, especially with George

Sand, to examine correspondence not as a mystical union, but as an experience of relation as exposure and disunity that we might say structures a kind of synaesthetic friendship. Compare the following definition from Giorgio Agamben's article, "Friendship": "Friendship is the instance of this concurrent perception of the friend's existence in the awareness of one's own existence. . . . The perception of existing is, in fact, always already divided up and shared or con-divided. Friendship names this sharing or con-division" (6). Liszt's visionary experience, as well as his correspondences, are modeled along the lines of this originary con-division, a shared synaesthetic perception of the other that communicates itself through him. With this in mind, I turn to his discussion of Raphael's St. Cecilia.

How does Liszt see Raphael's Saint Cecilia? His vision puts him in a passive position—he writes that he is "seized" with great force. He sees it both as a realization of human beauty, as a painting, and as a symbol of music. He writes, "Its abstract sense of line and its IDEAL gripped me as forcefully as did its beauty as a painting" (163). The painting stops short of being an allegory, for it actually represents its supersensible dimension—the angels singing above—on the same material plane as the earthly figure who aspires toward it. What music, and Liszt, capture in this moment is the threshold of signification that yet does not quite signify—the movement of symbolization itself that does not dissolve the material side of the symbol, but rather shows it "trembling" into the resonance of a nonmaterial meaning. "As she is about to rejoice in the glory of the Most High . . . her soul trembles with that same mysterious trembling that seized David when he played on his blessed harp" (163). This trembling of bodily materiality is echoed in the temporality of the painting as Liszt describes it: "One senses that her soul is no longer on earth, that her beautiful body is about to be transfigured." This threshold moment characterizes the visual aspect of music, the presence of its absence.

St. Cecilia is both the embodiment of the ideal and the figure who beholds or reaches up toward the ideal. She is both the means and the end of Liszt's musical vision. "Tell me, my friend, wouldn't you have seen in that noble figure, as I did, a symbol of music at the height of its power? Of art in its most spiritual and holy form: Isn't that virgin, ecstatically transported above reality, like the inspiration that sometimes fills an artist's heart—pure, true, full of insight, and unalloyed with mundane matters?" (163). She is both inspiration and the inspired one. Liszt describes, "Those eyes fixed on the vision, the unutterable rapture that floods her features . . . etc." She is both inspiration and discouragement, both attained and unattainable.

Let's take a step back and consider for a moment the figure of the Aeolian harp, which has been interpreted as a figure of the processes of perception and understanding. The Aeolian harp gained popularity during the Romantic period and is generally taken to be an important Romantic image.² One critic writes: "The supernatural, ghostly sound of these chords, changing, increasing and fading away with the wind without any player or any artificial contrivance, was wholly romantic." Often cited is M. H. Abrams essay "The Correspondent Breeze: A Romantic Metaphor" (1984), in which he writes: "The wind-harp has become a persistent romantic analogue of the poetic mind, the figurative mediator between outer motion and inner emotion. It is possible to speculate that, without this plaything of the eighteenth century, the Romantic poets would have lacked a conceptual model for the way the mind and imagination respond to the wind, so that some of their most characteristic passages might have been, in a literal sense, inconceivable."³ Abrams points out that the Aeolian harp not only links man and nature, but provides a model for thinking about this relationship as well. The Aeolian harp is a kind of technical supplement that would allow us to hear nature's own music, nature's own voice, directly; it is supposed to bring about precisely one of the moments of unity between man and nature for which Romanticism is famous. If we forget about the labor, the knowledge—the *techné*—implied in the construction of the harp, we hear only the resonance of this other. But if we attend to the framing device, we see that the animated resonance projected toward us is a momentary fiction supported by a surrounding narrative. The Aeolian harp, as a figure, presents not an immediate unity between self and other, humans and nature, but rather a temporary eclipse of separation that can only be articulated poetically—that is, in some manner figuratively, indirectly.

The Aeolian harp is itself a duplicitous object: both a material artifact and a poetic image. Aeolian harps, which were popular especially in England and Germany, are constructed by extending strings across some kind of box. The harp is then typically placed at a window, or more eccentrically, somewhere else where it can be stroked and played by the wind. Windows were the preferred place in England, while on the continent the harps were placed in gardens, grottoes, on medieval ruins, or between trees.⁴

The history of the Aeolian harp begins with the legend of David hanging his harp over his bed to catch the divine wind. This would indeed be divine inspiration. Athanasius Kircher, "a German polyhistorian, theologian and music theorist,"⁵ is credited with creating the first Aeolian harp in 1650. The instrument was connected to Aeolus, the god of the winds, by J. J.

Hoffmann in 1677.⁶ Following an article on the Aeolian harp published in 1781 (in W. Jones's *Physiological Disquisitions*), W. Jones took up production of the harp in cooperation with various London instrument makers. As Aeolian harps came into vogue toward the turn of the century, they were produced mostly in London and imported to the continent, especially to Germany. The playful experimentation with wind harps took place at the same time as a great deal of scientific research into the properties of sound in the eighteenth and nineteenth centuries.⁷

The Aeolian harp presents a kind of ambivalence between *techné* and nature that points to the persistence of a dual agency. On the one hand, there is a wish to submit to the tones of nature; in this sense, the inspired poet can be compared to the Aeolian harp, the passive conductor of a force beyond him- or herself. On the other hand, the technology required to allow the nature tones to resound gives control back to human agency.⁸ This ambivalence has been developed with wonderful clarity in the writings of E. T. A. Hoffmann, sometimes considered the first to write music criticism in the contemporary sense. It was Hoffmann who famously pronounced, "Music is the most romantic of all the arts." Hoffmann talks about the dualism of the Aeolian harp in terms of a "higher mechanics," contrasting normal sense with "higher" sense: "Can the music which dwells within us be any other than that which lies buried in nature as a profound mystery, comprehensible only by the inner higher sense, uttered by instruments, as the organs of it, merely in obedience to a mighty spell, of which we are the masters?"⁹ But insofar as "we" are masters of these tones, they are mediated by instruments and technique and only resound in analogy with the tones of nature. These can be generated only in the realm of dream, where mechanics, technology, and cause and effect are obliterated. The text continues to follow the conversation between the two characters, Ludwig and Ferdinand: "But in the purely psychical action and operation of the spirit—that is to say, in dreams—this spell is broken; and then, in the tones of familiar instruments, we are enabled to recognize those nature tones as wondrously engendered in the air, they come floating down to us, and swell and die away." "I am thinking of the Aeolian harp," said Ferdinand (98).¹⁰ The relation between conventional music and "nature tones" is one of metaphoric doubling. The "inner" or "higher" music is an elevated and rarified duplicate of the first. Once the rules of technology are broken, the "higher" music is reinscribed in conventional music, where it then resonates.

For Hoffmann, the experience of this kind of music decenters the self while connecting it with foreign elements. Here is one of the many descriptions he gives of musical ecstasy.

> As it [the music] rose in simple phrases, the clear upper notes like crystal bells, and sank till the rich low tones died away like the sighs of a despairing plaint, a rapture which words cannot describe took possession of me—the pain of a boundless longing seized my heart like a spasm. I could scarcely breathe, my whole being was merged in an inexpressible, superearthly delight. I did not dare to move; I could only listen; soul and body were merged in ear. (85)[11]

In this musical experience, the "I" contracts in a spasm, and body and soul are joined in the external organ of the ear.[12] It moves along with the wave of the swelling tone, rising and falling over time; its breath is suspended. The subject is like a vibrating string.[13] Like the tone of a string, its waves pass from outside to inside, from object to subject, through the organ of the ear. But what is the ear? It remains, like a frame, as a physical limit or condition that cannot ascend into the experience it makes possible. As it draws up, it also leads down. Likewise, as the text above continues, the poetic dream figure is interrupted by an obvious prosaic device. The narrator eventually falls asleep, and is awoken by "the shrill notes of a posthorn." The same organ takes apart what it joins. The post horn, a feature that occurs frequently in Hoffmann's prose, heralds the persistent return of the prosaic sphere of letters—of the technology of communication over time and space, delayed by delivery, distance, and difference.

I have given this exposition of these problems in Hoffmann because he is a prolific guru on the subject of musical experience as a loss of self in the medium of synaesthesia. Synaesthesia joins the senses, just as self and other, inside and outside, body and soul, are fused in the passages I have quoted.[14] Hoffmann's interest in the uncanny provides the interesting double of this musical experience. The uncanny duplicates the structure of possession by another, suspension of time and space and self-loss, but with the opposite values. The relation between music and the uncanny articulates the ambivalence around the exposure of the "I" to another—a contact that is both the consummation of the desire for union with an "other" and the fear of self-loss or death.[15] While musical instruments in general often figure this ambivalence, the image of the Aeolian harp exacerbates the tension outlined above since it puts the agency of the human subject and the "other" called Nature into direct rivalry.

Liszt's artistic vision clings to and reinforces the materiality that it would transcend, thus articulating the duality of the Aeolian harp. In George Sand's letter to Liszt of 1835, she outlines a strangely similar kind of vision in relation to Lavater's physiognomy. Johann Kaspar Lavater was an eighteenth-century Swiss writer most known for his work on physiognomy, the science of reading inner meaning or character through the external physical traits of the human form. Lavater, according to Sand, has a vision not unlike that of Saint Cecilia, or of the strange figure holding the magical harp. Even before developing the theory of physiognomy, which allows him to see inner traits in outer shapes, he has a kind of sixth sense regarding bodies. Sand describes how Lavater first became interested in physiognomy. Sand quotes Lavater: "Sometimes, at the first sight of certain faces, I felt a sort of quivering that lasted several instants after the departure of the person without my understanding the cause, or even without my thinking about the physiognomy that had produced it" (*Lettres d'un Voyageur*, 225). If the body itself gives way to a sense it manifests, the perceiving body likewise trembles into the physiognomic vision. Like Liszt, Lavater senses the trembling on the verge of meaning of a body that allows something to shine through. It is not clear whether this is a quality of the observer or the observed, a gift of vision of the observing physiognomist, or a quality of bodies and features that allows character to appear. Like the saint herself, Liszt and Lavater function as a kind of hinge between the sensible and the supersensible. As Sand describes it, Liszt gives way and himself becomes the trembling embodiment of a beyond: Sand writes to Liszt:

"For my part, I have always thought that certain organisms [*organisations*] are so exquisite that they possess almost divinatory faculties. In them, the terrestrial envelope is so ethereal, so diaphanous, so impressionable, that the spirit that animates them seems to see and penetrate across the matter that envelopes them or composes the external world. Their fibre is so tender and so loose that everything that escapes the coarse senses of other men makes it vibrate, just as the least breeze moves and makes tremble the strings of an Eolian harp. You must be one of the perfect and quasi-angelic organisms, my dear Franz" (225–26).

There is a kind of doubling of vision in the community of letters opened up between Liszt and Sand. Liszt is both absorbed into St. Cecilia and falls away from her. There is the same double valence in the quote from Shelley with which this chapter began. While at first he merely collects images, he then becomes inspired and fused with the figure of inspiration itself in the body of the saint. Likewise, Sand is drawn into the vibrating transparency of Liszt to hear the tones that are swept out of the Aeolian-harp-like frame, the music emerging from the sonorous body. In the same way, according to Sand, Lavater doubles the figure of Raphael, the perfection of whose images are mirrored in his own perfect form. Sand quotes Lavater saying: "'When I want to be filled with admiration for the perfection of the works of God, I have only to recall the form of Raphael.'" Sand continues: "This holy passion for the beautiful, since according to Lavater, true physical beauty is inseparable from the beauty of the soul, is expressed in many places in his book with the veritable naivete of an artist" (215).

"Quand je veux me remplir d'admiration pour la perfection des oeuvres de Dieu, je n'ai qu'à me rappeler la forme de Raphael.'" Sand continues: "Cette passion sainte pour le beau, parce que, selon Lavater, la vraie beauté physique et inséparable de la beauté de l'âme, s'exprime en plusieurs endroits de son livre avec une veritable naiveté d'artiste" (215).

Most importantly, this trembling vision is a figure of reading: "I both fear and respect those frail and nervous beings who live off electricity, and who seem to read in the mysteries of the supernatural world" (226) ("J'ai de crainte et de respect pour ces êtres frêles et nerveux aui vivent d'électricité, et qui semblent lire dans les mystères du monde surnaturel") (226). The perfection of the science of physiognomy will be nothing but a fulfilled hermeneutics of the figure, according to which the very shape of the body becomes a letter for reading the spirit of character.

"Eh bien," writes Sand, "Je n'en doute pas, l'homme en viendra un jour à pousser si loin l'examen de la forme humaine, qu'il lira les facultés et les penchants de son semblable comme dans un livre ouvert" (208). "So," writes Sand, "I have no doubt that man will someday succeed in pushing the study of human form so far that he will read the faculties and the tendencies of his fellow-man [son semblable] as in an open book" (208). Sand cites Lavater citing Herder, for her love of Germanic metaphor that sees physiognomic interpretation in terms of reading and writing: "'The forehead is the seat of serenity, of joy, of darkest pain, of anxiety, of stupidity, of ignorance and of evil. It is a bronze tablet in which all sentiments are engraved in characters of fire'" (210) ("'Le front est le siége de la sérénité, de la joie, du noir chagrin, de l'angoisse, de la stupidité, de l'ignorance et de la méchanceté. C'est une table d'airain oè tous les sentiments se gravent en caractères de feu'") (210).

What is reading, for Sand? Reading becomes a metaphor in which an animated figure is substituted for the letters on the page. Through readings, books themselves become personified. She writes,

> Je suis de ceux pour qui la connaissance d'un livre peut devenir un véritable événement moral. . . . Un livre a toujours été pour moi un ami, un conseil, un consolateur éloquent et calmes, dont je ne voulais pas epuiser vite les resources, et que je gardais pour les grandes occasions. (204–5)

> I am one of those people for whom knowing a book can become a veritable moral event. . . . For me, a book has always been a friend, an advisor, an eloquent and calm consoler, whose resources I would not want to exhaust quickly and which I would keep for big occasions. (204–5)

Sand's recollections of reading produce a genuine rhetorical transport: "Oh! Who among us does not recall with love the first works which he devoured and savoured!" ("Oh! Quel est celui de nous qui ne se rappelle avec amour les premiers ouvrages qu'il a dévorés ou savourés!") (205). Reading personifies the text into a wonderful friend and adviser. The mere contemplation of reading makes present again a scene of reading in the countryside. Sand recalls an afternoon, turning toward evening, when she is so absorbed in reading that she forgets the hour for dining and appears late for dinner to the forgiving reception by her grandmother. The ecstasy of reading carries the narrator away from her narrative and away from her addressee, just as Liszt regarding St. Cecilia, and St. Cecilia herself, are transported away from their surroundings. This narrative ecstasy gives way to the painting of a scene replete with details of the young Sand reading in a field; the past likewise gives way to the present tense in which the very characters of the text begin to disappear.

> "Oh! Que la nuit tombait vite sur ces pages divines! Que le crépuscule faisait cruellement flotter les caractères sur la feuille pâlissante! C'en est fait, les agneaux bêlent, les brebis sont arrivés à l'étable, le grillon prend possession des chaumes de la plaine. Les formes des arbres s'effacent dans le vague de l'air, comme tout à l'heure les caractères sur le livre. Il faut partir." (205)

> "Oh! How quickly night fell on those divine pages! How cruelly the twilight made the characters flutter on the paling page! . . . The shapes of the trees are erased in the wave of air, just as the characters on the book a moment ago. It's time to go."

The prose rises to the occasion, culminating in a series of vocative prosopopeias:

> Heureux temps! ô ma Vallée Noire, ô Corinne! ô Bernardin de Sainte-Pierre! ô l'Iliade! Ô Millevoye! ô Atala! ô les saules de la rivière! ô ma jeunesse écoulée! ô mon vieux chien qui n'oubliait pas l'heure du souper, et qui répondait au son lointain de la cloche par un douloureux hurlement de regret et de gourmandise! (206)

> Happy times! O my Vallee Noire, O Corinne! O Bernardin de Saint-Pierre! O the Iliad! Le Millevoye! O Atala! O the willows on the stream! O my departed youth! O my old dog who did not forget the supper hour and who responded to the distant sound of the bell with a painful howl of regret and gourmandise! (206)

Books become personified friends and companions, totally absorbing and distracting the narrator. "My God," Sand exclaims, "what was I saying? I wanted to tell you about Lavater" (206) ("Mon Dieu!" Sand exclaims, "que vous disais-je? Je voulais vous parler de Lavater").

The rhetorical amplification of reading is interrupted by the dinner bell; Sand's narrative, too, relinquishes its animated transport and returns to the deserted cottage. There, Sand finds a copy of Lavater's work and makes it her friend in isolation. The figures represented there and Lavater himself become living specters who keep her company in the empty house.

> Moi, je les vois sans cesse quand j'erre, le soir, das les vastes chambers obscures de ma maison déserte. Je vois derrière eux Lavater avec son regard clair et limpide, son nez pointu, indice de finesse et de pénétration, sa ressemblance ennoblie avec Érasme, son geste paternal. . . . je l'entends me dire, "Va, suis-les, tâche de leur ressembler, voilà tes maîtres, voilà tes guides; receuille leurs conseils, observe leurs préceptes, répète les formules saintes des leurs priers. (227–28)

> I see them incessantly as I wander about at evening in the vast dark rooms of my deserted house. I see behind them Lavater with his clear and limpid gaze, his pointed nose, an index of fine quality and penetration, his ennobled resemblance to Erasmus, his paternal gesture. . . . I hear him say to me: "Go, follow them,

try to resemble them, here are your masters, your guides; gather their advice, observe their precepts, repeat the holy formulas of their prayers." (227–28)

This ecstatic projection of subjectivity onto external read figures enacts rhetorically the ecstatic trembling of Saint Cecilia. Indeed, it overflows to produce a painting.

"And then," Sand continues, "I also see passing phantoms less imposing but full of grace or charm. These are my companions, these are my brothers. It is especially you, my dear Franz, whom I place in a painting [tableau] inundated with light, magical apparition that wells up in the darkness of my meditative evenings. . . . Yes young friend, yes, inspired artist, I understand this divine language but cannot speak it" (226). Sand conjures Liszt into this tableau in a friendship spoken in a mysterious language that neither can decipher ("Et puis," Sand continues, "Je vois passer aussi des fantômes moins imposants, mais plein de grâce ou de charme. Ce sont mes compagnons, ce sont mes frères. C'est vous surtout, mon cher Franz, que je place dans un tableau inondé de lumière, apparition magique qui surgit dans les ténèbres de mes soirées méditatives. . . . Oui jeune ami, oui, artiste inspiré, je comprends cette langue divine et ne puis la parler") (228). Sand describes music not only as the language of friendship, but as friendship itself; not simply communication, but communicability per se.

> The musician lives on chords, on sympathy and union with his students and his executors. Music is taught, reveals itself, spreads itself out, communicates itself [s'enseigne, se revele, se répond, se communique.] Does not the harmony of sounds demand a harmony of wills and sentiments? What a superb republic is realized by 100 instrumentalists joined together by a single spirit of order and love to execute a symphony of the great master! . . . Yes, music is prayer, it is faith, it is friendship, it is association par excellence. (196)

Music and its vision are established through multiples, not individuals. On the page, Liszt and Sand abut and intertwine to allow their common vision to emerge; not a vision held in common, but vision as a separation and doubling, a transcending and remaining, an ecstatic impulse and return. Liszt responds to Sand:

> The republic of music, already established by a leap of your

young imagination, is still only a dream for me. . . . And when I reflect seriously on my life, I blush with shame and confusion to pit your dreams against my realities;—the heavenly flames with which your poetic fancy encircles my brow, against the earthly dust my steps raise on the mundane road I travel;—your noble presentiments, your beautiful illusions . . . against the gloomy discouragement that sometimes seizes me when I compare the impotence of the effort with the eagerness of the desire, the nothingness of the work with the limitlessness of the idea—those miracles of understanding and regeneration wrought by the thrice-blessed lyre of ancient times, against the sad and sterile role to which it is seemingly confined today (4–5).

Liszt's voice thus comes forth as one of difference and dissolution. The relationality of Sand and Liszt—the alternating tones—recalls the duplicity of Liszt's vision of himself with which this chapter began—a duplicity that mirrors or echoes the dualism of the figure of the Aeolian harp. Both congruent with nature and a human-made instrument, it simultaneously invokes and demystifies the image of inspiration.

Chapter 3

Baudelaire's Synaesthesia

Baudelaire's statement: "Créer un poncif—c'est le génie" ("To create a cliché—that is genius") is well known and has itself perhaps become a cliché. But besides this, perhaps his greatest creation, and common place, is the figure of synaesthesia/correspondence, possibly the most worn-out trademark of his poetry as a foundational symbolist work. Baudelaire himself points to the used-up quality of *correspondance* in the prose poem, "L'Invitation au Voyage." Referring to a composition by Carl Maria von Weber, Baudelaire writes, "Un musicien a écrit *l'Invitation à la Valse*; quel est celui qui composera *l'Invitation au Voyage*?" (*OC*, 1: 302; cf. commentary, *OC*, 1:1324) ("A musician has written *Invitation to the Waltz*; who will compose *Invitation to the voyage*?") (*Paris Spleen*, 33). While inverting the terms, *writing* and *composing*, the prefabricated sense of the invitation is registered in the italics, calling for Baudelaire's own text or the lyric poem of the same title. Just as the mystical alchemists, as in the writings of Balzac, have maneuvered in the realm of spiritual correspondence, horticultural mystics have prefigured the flowers that the speaker claims as his own: "Qu'ils cherchent, qu'ils cherchent encore, qu'ils reculent sans cesse les limites de leur bonheur, ces alchimistes de l'horticulture! Qu'ils proposent des prix de soixante et de cent mile florins pour qui résoudra leurs ambitieux problems! Moi, j'ai trouvé ma *tulipe noire* et mon *dahlia bleu*!" (*OC*, 1: 303) ("Let them search and continue to search, ceaselessly to push back their happiness limit—alchemists of horticulture! Let them offer sixty or a hundred thousand florins to someone who can solve their difficult problems! As for me, I have found my *black tulip* and my *blue dahlia*") (*Paris Spleen*, 33). The speaker's unique findings reference the material experiments of contemporary *tulpomanie*, while the italics register the used quality of the names of his flowers: Dumas's novel *La Tulipe Noir* and Pierre Dupont's popular song, *Le Dahlia Bleu* (*OC*, 1: 1324). Plucked from literature and music, these flowers become allegorical.

> Fleur incomparable, tulipe retrouvée, allégorique dahlia, c'est là, n'est-ce pas, dans ce beau pays si calme et si rêveur, qu'il faudrait aller vivre et fleurir? Ne serais-tu pas encadrée dans ton analogie, et ne pourrais-tu pas te mirer, pour parler comme les mystiques, dans ta propre *correspondance*? (*OC*, 1: 303)

> Incomparable flower, retraced tulip, dahlia of allegory, is it not there, in that fair land so calm and dreamlike, we must go in order to live and to flower? Would you not step into your analogy; could you not see yourself in—as the mystics put it—your own proper *correspondence*? (*SP*, 34)

The speaker emulates others in speaking of *correspondance*, the italics again indicating the clichéd quality of the common place of correspondence, the poetic "pays de Cocaigne."[1]

Despite the used and used-up nature of the language of *correspondance*, an earlier generation of critics hailed it as a poetic achievement. In the meantime, correspondence has fallen out of critical favor as a figure of unity and harmony in the service of "the ideal." Critical attention over the last several decades has instead shifted to those dislocating features foregrounding difference and distance—whether that be the focus on prose against lyric, "spleen," differentiation, sexuality, destruction, nonidentity. This is accompanied by an investment in Baudelaire's rejection of what is called "Romanticism" as a figure of ideal unity. In her article, "Inhuman Beauty: Baudelaire's Bad Sex," Elissa Marder points to the way in which readings of Baudelaire have tended to be polarized: "Many of his [Baudelaire's] readers opt for either flowers over evil (in which case Baudelaire becomes a poet of synesthesia and harmonious 'correpondances') or evil over flowers (in which case Baudelaire becomes a libertine poet of sin, sexuality, freedom, and the Devil). . . . The very gesture of choosing between spleen and idéal, as it were, often accompanies and produces reading practices that reinforce tired moralisms and worn-out homilies and neutralize the very aspects of Baudelaire's poetry that are the most forceful, the most inimitable, the most enduring, and the most subversive."[2] Instead, Marder argues that Baudelaire's "bad sex"—his "impotence, his perversions, his fetishism, his misogyny, his hatred of childbirth, and his celebration of sexual cruelty would hold no interest . . . had they not profoundly altered and transformed . . . the very foundations of poetic language and very experience of what constitutes poetic beauty" (8). She seeks to read the intertwining of "*Fleurs*" and "*mal*," rather than their binary opposition, through the lens of "bad sex." Need synaesthesia and *correspondances* be sequestered at the binary pole of ideal? Others have suggested that the "system" of correspondence is itself ambiguous, inclined toward a certain transcendence and unification, on the one hand, but tending, in its connection with modernity, toward a disarticulation of that very unification on the other.[3] Synaesthesia, as I have been arguing, seems to unify the senses but actually holds them apart in its horizontal articulation.

While Swedenborg and Fourier are traditionally identified as sources for the mystical theory of correspondence(s) and "l'analogie universelle," it is unclear how much Baudelaire actually read either of them.[4] Walter Benjamin, along with Proust, sets aside the "gelehrte Schrifttum über die correspondances (sie sind Gemeingut der Mystiker; Baudelaire ist bei Fourier auf sie gestoßen)" (*GS*, 1.2: 638) ("the scholarly literature on *correspondances* [the common property of mystics; Baudelaire encountered them in Fourier's writings]") (*Selected Writings*, 4:333). The correspondences, for Benjamin, involve a coming together of prehistory and the present in the shape of *Erfahrung*. "Was Baudelaire mit den correspondances im Sinn hatte, kann als eine Erfahrung bezeichnet werden, die sich krisensicher zu etablieren sucht" (638) ("What Baudelaire meant by *correspondances* can be described as an experience which seeks to establish itself in crisis-proof form") (*SW*, 4:333). And further: "Die correspondances sind die Data des Eingedenkens. Sie sind keine historischen, sondern Data der Vorgeschichte" (639) ("*Correspondances* are the data of recollection—not historical data, but data of prehistory") (*SW*, 334). Synaesthesia is an event not really of sense perception, but of memory (*PW*, 464). The "correspondance au ciel" (correspondence with heaven) is translated into a "correspondance au/du passé," correspondence with/of the past.

The situation of *correspondances* is this: it brings together past and present without merging them, that is, it dissolves *Erlebnis* into *Erfahrung*. *Correspondance* is temporally riven, broken. Benjamin tells us: "Simultane Korrespondenzen . . . gibt es nicht. Vergangenes murmelt in den Entsprechungen mit" (640) ("There are no simultaneous correspondences . . . What is past murmurs in the correspondences") (*SW*, 4:334). The interplay of *Erlebnis* and *Erfahrung*[5] brings correspondence into the proximity of constellation and the dialectical image, as in the famous passage in the *Passagen Werk*.

> Nicht ist es so, daß das Vergangene sein Licht auf das Gegenwärtige oder das Gegenwärtige sein Licht auf des Vergangne wirft, sondern das Bild ist dasjenige, worin das Gewesene mit dem Jetzt blitzhaft zu einer Konstellation zusammen tritt. (*PW*, N3, 1: 578)

> It is not that what is past casts its light on what is present, or what is present its light on the past; rather, image is that wherein what has been comes together in a flash with the now to form a constellation. (*AP*, 463)

Partaking in all the qualities of the constellation, correspondence(s) would be a fundamentally spread out and differentiated unity, not a transcendent totalization—a unity rhythmic rather than static. Baudelaire's work gathers and transfigures time but does not outdo it. Thus it rhythmically alternates between the workaday days of the calendar, and the holidays, the thick and pregnant time, that falls out of it (642–43)—between spleen and ideal. Correspondences—or "*Correspondances*"—are not isolated on one side of this binary, but actually stretch out between the two poles.[6] This stretching might constitute a sort of middle as Zachary Sng has discussed it in *Middling Romanticism*.

What exactly is the relationship between correspondence(s) and synaesthesia? Some ally correspondence with the "vertical" axis connecting material and spiritual signs, contrasted with the "horizontal" axis of synaesthesia, connecting the various senses to each other. Paul Gordon is right to see them as intertwined, and writes of "synaesthetic correspondences" characterizing not only "Correpondances," but all of "*Les Fleurs du Mal*."[7]

Correspondence(s), I would like to suggest, is something like the condition of possibility of synaesthesia; Benjamin considers them as the *medium*, and the meaningful substratum, of synaesthesia. He writes,

> Es wäre ein Irrtum, die Erfahrung, die in den correspondances beschlossen liegt, als planes Gegenstück zu gewissen Experimenten zu denken, die man mit der Synaesthesie (dem Farbenhören oder Tonsehen) in psychologischen Laboratorien angestellt hat. Bei Baudelaire handelt es sich weniger um die bekannten

Reaktionen, aus denen die schöngeistigen oder snobistische Kunstkritik soviel Wesens gemacht hat als um das Medium, in dem solche Reaktionen erfolgen. Dieses Medium ist die Erinnerung und sie war bei ihm von ungewöhnlicher Dichtigkeit. Die korrespondierenden Sinnesdaten korrespondieren in ihr; sie sind geschwängert mit Erinnerungen, die so dicht heranfluten, daß sie nicht aus diesem Leben sondern aus einer geräumigen vie antérieure herzustammen scheinen. Auf dieses Leben spielen die regards familiers an, mit der solche Erfahrungen den Betroffnen ansehen. (*PW* J 79, 6; 464)

It would be an error to think of the experience contained in the *correspondances* as a simple counterpart to certain experiments with synesthesia (with hearing colors or seeing sounds) that have been conducted in psychologists' laboratories. In Baudelaire's case, it is a matter less of the well-known reactions, about which effete or snobbish art criticism has made such a fuss, than of the medium in which such reactions occur. This medium is the memory, and with Baudelaire it was possessed of unusual density. The corresponding sensory data correspond in it; they are teeming with memories, which run so thick that they seem to have arisen not from this life at all but from some more spacious *vie antérieure*. It is this prior existence that is intimated by the 'familiar eyes' with which such experiences scrutinize the one who has them. (*AP*, 367)

Understood in this way, correspondence and synaesthesia cannot be separated and opposed, but rather they intermingle and interrupt one another.

Jonathan Culler, for his part, reads correspondence as a figure for intertextuality that grounds an in-depth reading of precursor poems.[8] Correspondence subtends the resonance among texts, as well as the explanatory reverberation that allows remarks from Baudelaire's prose to be applied in interpretations of his poetry. Correspondence is thus both a hallmark of Baudelaire's individuality, and a sort of "Gemeingut," to use Benjamin's term, that connects him with others—both literary influences and critical responses. Many have pointed out that Baudelaire consistently turns to others to ground both the theory of correspondence and the poem "Correspondances." There is a kind of oscillation between singular and plural, or as Baudelaire might say, of solitude and multitude.[9] In the *Passagen-Werk*,

Benjamin points again and again to Baudelaire's loneliness and status as a loner; yet we can also read, through synaesthesia, his participation in what Kevin McLaughlin calls a "strange community."[10] It is a community based not on the presence to each other of multiple pre-existing subjects, but rather as oblique presences invoked and exposed to each other by reading and citation—thus a "philological community."

"Richard Wagner and Tannäuser in Paris" (1861) is Baudelaire's only critical text devoted to music. Despite his admitted ignorance of music, the poet admired and identified with the composer. He found in Wagner a fellow translator of the soul.[11] He describes this performance of translation in synaesthetic terms, combining Wagner's music with color and painting. Baudelaire writes,

> Aucun musicien n'excelle, comme Wagner, à peindre l'espace et la profondeur, matériels et spirituels. . . . Il possède l'art de traduire, par des gradations subtiles, tout ce qu'il y a d'excessif, d'immense, d'ambitieux, dans l'homme spirituel et naturel. Il semble parfois, en écoutant cette musique ardente et despotique, qu'on retrouve peintes sur le fond des ténèbres, déchiré par la rêverie, les vertigineuses conceptions de l'opium. (*OC*, 2: 785)

> No musician excels as Wagner does in painting space and depth, both material and spiritual. . . . He possesses the art of translating, by means of the subtlest shades, all that is excessive, immense and ambitious in spiritual and natural man. One seems sometimes, when listening to this fiery and peremptory music, to recapture the dizzy perceptions of an opium dream, painted upon a backcloth or canvas of darkness. (*Painter of Modern Life*, 117)

Baudelaire explains that he has found in Wagner's music an articulation of his own theory of correspondence. He describes his reaction to Wagner's music as follows:

> M'est-il permis à moi-même de raconter, de rendre avec des paroles la traduction inevitable que mon imagination fit du même morceau, lorsque je l'entendis pour la première fois, les yeux fermés, et que je me sentis pour ainsi dire enlevé de terre? . . . Ce qui serait vraiment surprenant, c'est que le son *ne pût pas* suggérer la couleur, que les couleurs *ne pussent pas* donner l'idée d'une mélodie, et que le son et la couleur fussent

impropres à traduire des idées; les s'étant toujours exprimées par une analogie réciproque, depuis le jour où Dieu a proféré le monde comme une complexe et indivisible totalité. (*OC*, 2: 698)

May I now be permitted to describe, to convey in words the inevitable translation made by my own imagination of the same piece when I heard it for the first time, with my eyes closed, feeling, as it were, lifted from the earth? . . . What would be truly surprising would be to find that sound *could not* suggest colour, that colours *could not* evoke the idea of a melody, and that sound and colour were *unsuitable* for the translation of ideas, seeing that things have always found their expression through a system of reciprocal analogy ever since the day when God uttered the world like a complex and indivisible totality. (116)

As his own translation or painting, Baudelaire then offers the first two stanzas of his poem, "Correspondances."

La nature est un temple où de vivants piliers
Laissent parfois sortir de confuses paroles;
L'homme y passe à travers des forêts de symbols
Qui l'observent avec des regards familiers.

Comme de longs échos qui de loin se confondent
Dans une ténébreuse et profonde unité,
Vaste comme la nuit et comme la clarté,
Les parfums, les couleurs et les sons se répondent.
(*OC*, 2: 78)

Nature is a temple whose columns are alive and sometimes issue disjointed messages. We thread our way through a forest of symbols that peer out, as if recognizing us.

Like long echoes from far away, merging into a deep dark unity, vast as night, vast as the light, smells and colors and sounds concur. (*Flowers of Evil*, 14)

Baudelaire inscribes in the essay his own poem, "Correspondances," as a translation of Wagner's music. The figure of synaesthesia joins the senses, while the understanding of art as translation and correspondence joins different artists in a citational community. Similarly, in the *Salon de 1846*, Baudelaire finds the theory of correspondence in a passage he quotes from E. T. A. Hoffmann that presents the crossing of the senses: "Une analogie et une réunion intime entre les couleurs, les sons et les parfums" (*OC*, 2: 425) ("The analogy and intimate reunion of colors, sounds and perfumes"). The commingling of citation, translation, and synaesthesia sets up "correspondences" among fellow artists.[12]

Walter Benjamin has remarked on the strangeness of Paul Valéry's remark that "Baudelaire's problem . . . might have—indeed must have—posed itself in these terms: "How to be a great poet, but neither Lamartine, nor Hugo nor Musset." This problem, Valéry says, "was essentially Baudelaire. It was his raison d'État."[13] If Baudelaire emerges, for Valéry, from a series of proper names, his notion of community, too, arises out of a series of names. The community that comes into being in this way is not a group of psychological subjects, but rather is a collection of terms that are held apart even as they are grouped together. What connects them does so alogically through the materiality of language; it not only connects, but also fragments, serializes, expands, and realigns. The simple stating and exposure of proper names takes up the space through which a sort of community spreads itself. But this type of synaesthesia or community does not gather together presences or aggregate individuals through presence into a whole. Rather, through resonance and dislocation, to use the language of Jean-Luc Nancy, each singular plural—the many singulars—are exposed, set out, and brought into play. Against this backdrop of the wide-ranging discourse on community I turn to the old, or perhaps the new old, question of synaesthesia in Baudelaire.

The proper names punctuating Baudelaire's writing sets up a communicative network drawing together singulars into a common project. The unity of the arts emerges as an immense correspondence. I recall the communicative reciprocity of the famous sonnet quoted above. In the first stanza, nature and art speak together the symbolic language that animates architectural elements and mirrors man back to himself.

> La Nature est un temple où de vivants piliers
> Laissent parfois sortir de confuses paroles;
> L'homme y passe à travers des forêts de symboles
> Qui l'oberservent avec des regards familiers.

Nature is a temple whose columns are alive and sometimes issue disjointed messages. We thread our way through a forest of symbols that peer out, as if recognizing us. (*Flowers of Evil*, 14)

Emanating resonances join and fuse, "into a unity obscure and profound" ("dans une ténébreuse et profonde unité"). These Pythagorean overtones resonate and overlap, bringing into vibration a cosmic unity of sympathetic ratios. The figure of synaesthesia follows, joining the senses in a relation of reciprocal response:

The perfumes, colors, and sounds correspond.

Les parfums, les couleurs, et les sons se répondent.

First, "comme," a conjunction meaning "like" or "as," works to join the disaggregated senses: "doux comme les hautbois, verts comme les prairies."[14] "Mellow as oboes, green as prairies." Yet even here, the comparisons are not quite smooth or symmetrical; the perfumes of the child are sweet or soft like oboes, and green like prairies. The first figure crosses smell and sound, the second connects smell and color. Sweet must refer indirectly to the sound of the oboe—not the oboe itself—while green is a direct attribute of the prairies.[15] The "*vert*" of "green" suggests the word *vers*, meaning verse. Baudelaire's green verse opens up as the prairie, the verdant ground on which flowers and correspondences grow. Green verse turns over (*verser*) the property of color into the space of writing (*verser*). *Vers*, in its adverbial sense of "toward," also enacts the movement upward that elevates synaesthesia into correspondence articulated in the final line, "qui chantent les transports de l'esprit et des sens" ("that sing the transports of spirit and the senses").

These three senses of *vers*/*vert*, unrelated etymologically and thus connected only by the chance qualities of the sound of the word, adjoin in the poem, "Le Soleil" ("The Sun"), in which we might also think of the word *vers*, meaning "worm":

Ce père nourricier, ennemi des chloroses,
Éveille dans les champs les vers comme les roses;
Il fait s'évaporer les soucis vers le ciel . . .
Et commande aux moissons de croître et de mûrir
Dans le Coeur immortel qui toujours veut fleurir! (*OC*, 1: 83)

> This foster father, enemy of chlorosis, makes verse/worms spring like roses from the fields; makes care evaporate into air . . . and commands the harvest to increase and ripen, within the immortal spirit willing always to flower. (*Flowers of Evil*, 112)

Verse arises like roses thanks to the enemy of chlorosis: both a fading of green, and a becoming green. According to Webster's, chlorosis is both "an iron-deficiency anemia [especially of adolescent girls] that may impart a greenish tint to the skin—called also *greensickness* 2: a diseased condition in green plants marked by yellowing or blanching." As the sun descends, cares evaporate into the sky, "vers le ciel," green, toward or verse the sky (a senseless syntax). The working of "vers" here might be called an "unworking," a "désouevrement," that dismembers the text here just as rejuvenation and transcendence are invoked thematically. Cares and flowers rise up as the sun comes down into the cities. The immortal heart replaces the field (*champs*) of flowers as the place forever flowering, or at least forever wanting to flower.

The heart flowers in its commanding exposure to the sun; it must be stimulated by something other than itself. Even in its solitude, poetic voice is incited through the address of another and thus is already many. Like the rays of the sun, the gaze of—the beautiful woman?—incites the flowering of verse, as in the poem: "What will you say this evening, poor solitary soul" ("Que diras-tu ce soir, pauvre âme solitaire"), which continues,

> Que diras-tu, mon coeur, coeur autrefois flétri,
> A la très belle, à la très bonne, à la très chère,
> Dont le regard divin t'a soudain refleuri? (*OC*, 1: 43)

> What will you say, my heart, heart withered long-ago, to the most-beautiful, the most-good, the most-cherished, from whose divine glance you have suddenly flowered again? (57)

The self-address of poetic voice here sets up a conversation among the speaker, the soul, and the heart, dispersing and multiplying what would be an "I"—but no "I" is ever enunciated in the poem. The foregrounding of the heart in the second line syncopates the articulation of voice: the even alexandrine of the first line is disrupted, stumbles, and stutters over the direct address, commas, and repetition of the word *coeur* ("heart"). But the evenness resumes, gathering together the spiritual flesh, the perfume, the eye, the clarity, in a loose synaesthesia: "Sa chair spirituelle a le parfum des

Anges, / et son oeil nous revêt d'un habit de clarté" (ll. 7–8) ("Her spiritual flesh has the perfume of Angels / and her eye clothes us anew in a garment of light") (57). The rhythm of the poem gathers force and accelerates as the syntax detaches from the indicative and rises in the repeated subjunctives joining and reversing singularity and plurality.

> Que ce soit dans la nuit et dans la solitude,
> Que ce soit dans la rue et dans la multitude,
> Son fantôme dans l'air danse comme un flambeau. (*OC*, 1: 43)

> Whether in night and solitary, whether in the street among a multitude, her apparition dances in the air like a torch. (57)

This rising up breaks off in the appearance of a figure, "son fantôme," "her phantom," which then speaks as the voice of the Muse—the ultimate figure of inspiration and incitation through and by another.

The preceding poem, "Tout Entière," enacts a similar dialogue. A demon, or "The Demon," comes to the speaker, enunciated only indirectly as "me" (both direct and indirect object), and asks which compositional element of enchantment, of "her body," is most pleasing. The voice exclaims, "O mon âme! / Tu répondis à l'Abhorré" (*OC*, 1: 42) ("Oh my soul! You replied to the Shunned one") (56), and then quotes the soul's speech proferred over the next three and half stanzas. This personified fragment of the self, the soul who is speaking, articulates the unity of the figure asked about through synaesthesia.

> Ô métamorphose mystique
> De tous mes sens fondues en un!
> Son haleine fait la musique,
> Comme sa voix fait le parfum! (42)

> O mystic metamorphosis, melding all my senses into one! Her breath makes music, as her voice gives off perfume! (56)

The speaker claims to be seduced by this figure, and resounds in unison with it—a unison beyond analysis or decomposition.

> Et l'harmonie est trop exquise,
> Qui gouverne tout son beau corps,

> Pour que l'impuissante analyse
> En note les nombreux accords. (42)

> And the harmony that governs her beautiful body as a whole
> is too exquisite for an impotent analysis to distinguish the
> multilayered chords. (56)

Synaesthesia, though, keeps the senses apart syntactically even as it thematizes their fusion. The speaking soul becomes here a painter, framing the figure it presents; likewise, it remains distinct from the "me" and the Demon with whom it converses.[16]

Synaesthesia opens up the dispersion of the senses that makes fusion, combination, organization, and community possible. These poetic dialogues, whether among parts of the self or between the self and its Muse/Demon, present the exposure of one speaker position to another; they do not present a realistic or psychological representation of intersubjectivity. Artistic community, for Baudelaire, consists in this syncopation of self that distends identity at the same time that it allows for resonance, concord, and discord. Baudelaire's singular identity emerges as a point in a multiplex network of names joined and dissociated by the rhythms and syncopations of synaesthesia. The "I" falls out of the harmony of the spheres, as in "L'Heauton timoroumenos," where the speaker asks the following:

> Ne suis-je pas un faux accord/Dans le divin symphonie,
> Grâce à la vorace Ironie
> Qui me secoue et qui me mord? (*OC*, 1: 78)

> Am I not a discord in the divine symphony, thanks to voracious
> Irony who shakes me and bites me? (105)

The harmonious vibrations of correspondence draw back, here, into bodily spasms and percussions heralding violence and battle.

> Tes chers sanglots retentiront
> Comme un tambour qui bat la charge! (78)

> Your precious sobs will pound out like the drumbeat for a
> charge! (105)

The eternal laughter invoked in the final stanza echoes the quaking of the shaken body, the battered tambourine, and the resounding sobs. The sense of spirit or identity is punctured and punctuated in intermittence with the body, extending in a nonself identical relation of self-affection.

> Je suis la plaie et le couteau! . . .
> la victime et le bourreau! (79)

> I am the wound and the knife! . . . victim and hangman. (105)

These lines specify and take apart the two parts of the Greek work forming the title: *heauton timoroumenos*, the tormentor of oneself. The term is borrowed from a comedy by Terence. According to the Pléiade, it was used by De Quincey and in a letter from St. Beuve that Baudelaire would not have known (*OC*, 1:985). The intertextual resonance thus enacts the identification and differentiation that the term puts into place.

Baudelaire's writing is peopled by correspondences—letters addressed to and from mouthpieces whose lips break out in the laughter of the unity of the arts—a unity unsubstantial, never present, constituted in the crossing over of senses. According to Baudelaire, the poetics of synaesthesia and correspondence distinguish Victor Hugo as the universal artist whose verse combines the arts of poetry, music, sculpture, and painting.

> La musique des vers de Victor Hugo s'adapte aux profondes harmonies de la nature; sculpteur, il découpe dans ses strophes la forme inoubliable des choses; peintre, il les illumine de leur couleur proper. (2: 132)

> The music of Victor Hugo's verse adapts to nature's most profound harmonies; a sculptor, he carves out in his strophes the unforgettable form of things; a painter, he illuminates them with their own color." (My translation)

The grafting of the particular arts onto each other marks out the limits and planes of exposure between the various media, just as the line, "Perfumes, colors and sounds correspond" ("les parfums, les couleurs et les sons se répondent") holds apart the singular terms it puts into communication. Correspondence takes place as this mutual exposure. The persistence of proper names—concrete singularities that cannot be subsumed into a concept or whole—parallels the irreducible resilience of the senses in language. "Les Phares," "Beacon Lights" (two poems after "Correspondances"), presents a string of artists marking out relay points on a vast network across time and space. The first eight stanzas are punctuated each one by a proper name: Rubens, Leonardo da Vinci, Rembrandt, Michelangelo, Puget, Watteau, Goya, and Delacroix. The stanzas present series of images only loosely connected to the proper name with which they are grouped. Each artist's name gives rise to a set of associations, but remains syntactically free. For example,

> Rubens, fleuve d'oubli, jardin de la paresses . . . Léonard de Vinci, miroir profound . . . Goya, cauchemar plein de choses inconnues . . . Delacroix, lac de sang hanté des mauvais anges . . . (*OC*, 1: 13–14)

> Rubens, river of oblivion, garden of laziness . . . Da Vinci, deep dark mirror . . . Goya, bald nightmare of things unknown . . . Delacroix, lake of blood, haunted by evil angels . . . (16)

The names hang suspended, as if they were apostrophes, but end up being rather the first term in an apposition. Their placement, followed by a comma, installs a syncopated scansion. No system organizes this list. The names open up spaces, as just quoted, but most notably perhaps, "Michel-Ange, lieu vague ou l'on voit des Hercules / Se mêler à des Christs . . ." ("Michelangelo, vague area where various Hercules are seen . . .") (16). A name is a stanza—a room, in Italian—a garden, a vague place. This is strange, to call an artist a "vague place." Similarly, the Delacroix stanza opens up a tableau-like scenario: "Delacroix, lac de sang hanté des mauvais anges . . ." (13) ("Delacroix, lake of blood haunted by evil angels") (*OC*, 1: 13–14). There is a special relationship between Baudelaire and Delacroix, about whom he wrote several texts. This relationship is marked in the stanza on Delacroix by the intrusion of poetry, *vers*, verse, the homonym of *vert*, green, in the Delacroix scene: "un bois de sapins vert," a forest of evergreen fir. But the green poetry is strange, picked up in the following line by "des fanfares étranges" ("strange fanfares") and rhyming vaguely with another proper name, "comme un soupir étouffé de Weber" ("like a stifled sigh from Weber").

The ninth stanza presents another list, this time of expressive gestures, with the demonstrative pronoun that suggests a reference still only intimated:

"ces malédictions, ces blasphèmes, ces plaintes, / ces extases, ces cris, ces pleurs, ces *Te Deum* . . ." ("These curses, these blasphemies, groans, ecstasies, cries, these tears, these Te Deums . . ."). This repetitive enumeration gathers together the various artistic enunciations in a resounding sound wave, the "echo rehearsed in a thousand labyrinths" ("écho redit par mille labyrinths"). Community is established through repetition and echo, resaying and resounding: redit, répété, renvoyé, Mille sentinelles, mille porte-voix, mille citadelles" ("a thousand sentinals, a thousand megaphones, a thousand citadels"), voices resounding trying to find one another—"A call to hunters lost in the wood" ("Un appel de chasseurs perdus dans les grands bois"). Here we are reminded of the inverse correspondence of "Obsession," which might be read as one such cry.[17] It begins: "Grands bois, vous m'effrayez comme des cathédrals" (75) ("Forests, you frighten me, as do cathedrals") (101). Here the speaker is haunted, rather than comforted, by the returning echoes of the plaints of others (in particular, of course, De Quincey— "les échos de vos de Profundis," "the echoes of your de Profundis"). The hypersignificance of an already made nature, an already populated exterior, threatens the originality of the poetic voice, itself now only an echo of an other.

> Je te hais, Océan! Tes bonds et tes tumults,
> Mon esprit les retrouve en lui; ce rire amer
> De l'homme vaincu, plein de sanglots et d'insultes,
> Je l'entends dans le rire énorme de la mer. (*OC*, 1: 75)

> You I hate, Ocean! Your bounding and your tumult I find again in my mind; that bitter laugh of the beaten man, full of sobs and insults, I hear it in the sea's enormous laughter. (101)

The personified universe—the mono-verse, the single poem—draws the speaker into an overly mediated linguistic context.

> Comme tu me plairais, ô nuit! Sans ces étoiles
> Dont la lumière parle un langage connu!
> Car je cherche le vide, et le noir, et le nu! (*OC*, 1: 75)

> How you would please me, O night! But for those stars whose light speaks a known language! For I seek the void, the dark, the naked! (101)

The speaker finds comfort in the decomposition of its terms: the *nu* rather than the *connu*, the *toile* rather than the *étoile*. Refigured as painting, the darkness is populated instead by the lost sparks of the speaker's own perceptions.

> Mais les ténèbres sont elles-mêmes des toiles
> Où vivent, jaillisant de mon oeil par milliers,
> Des êtres disparus aux regards familiers. (*OC*, 1: 76)

> But shadows themselves are canvases where, welling from my eye
> by thousands, beings long vanished live, with familiar gaze. (101)

The celestial dissemination of these "milliers," linked with the cast of thousands of "Beacon Lights," both connects and renders strange the stars and the eyes of the I. The familiarity of the language of others is muffled; the life of these disappeared beings is syncopated: they live, having disappeared; perhaps they live on. The line is suggestive of the strange syncopations that allows for the possibility that we see a star already burned out, or that the message emitted is received only by the one who has forgotten its code.

If correspondence sets up a kind of community here, it is not articulated through any sort of full presence or coming together of individual entities, but through the syncopated exposure of rhythms to each other. We do not have here the calm mirroring of the self in itself—as in the first verse of "les Phares," "Comme l'air dans le ciel et la mer dans la mer" ("like air in the atmosphere and sea in the sea") (16)—but instead the self-differentiating rending of the ocean and its antagonistic relation to the speaker. In the quatrain quoted earlier, man and sea are linked by the quaking of laughter—"rire amer, rire de la mer," and the heaving of sobs. Similarly, in the final stanza of "Beacon Lights," the sob connects artists through the ages, heaving up the spasm of finitude as it breaks against its own limit.

> Que cet ardent sanglot qui roule d'âge en âge
> Et vient mourir au bord de votre éternité. (*OC*, 1: 14)

> This fervent sob that rolls from age to age, to die at the brink
> of your eternity! (17)

Recall that Delacroix's place in "Les Phares" is characterized by a play of red and green, the blood-lake and the green pines, which gives rise to the strange fanfares of Weber.[18] In "On Color," published in the 1846 *Salon*, Baudelaire traces out a similar generation of music out of color. The text lays out a space in which colors and elements extend and interact to emit energy and sound: "Supposons un bel espace de nature où tout verdoie, rougeoie, poudroie en pleine liberté," Baudelaire writes,

> Let us suppose a beautiful natural space where everything turns green, red, dusty or iridescent as it wishes . . . where everything is in a state of perpetual vibration which causes lines to tremble and fulfils the law of eternal and universal movement (*Art in Paris* 48), "où toutes choses, diversement colorées suivant leur constitution . . . se trouvent en perpétuelle vibration, laquelle fait trembler les lignes et complète la loi du movement éternel et universel. (*OC*, 2: 422).

> Where all things, variously coloured in accordance with their molecular structure . . . is in a state of perpetual vibration which causes lines to tremble and fulfils the law of eternal and universal movement. (48)

The verbalization of the color names embeds them in the horizontal spacing of syntax and writing. Next, an alternation between blue and green extends: "It is the sea," Baudelaire writes. Objects are then articulated in green resonance with the greening of the opening sentence (*tout verdoie*):

> The trees are green, the grass and the moss are green; the tree-trunks are snaked with green, and the unripe stalks are green; green is nature's ground-bass, because green marries easily with all the other colours. (48)

> Les arbres sont verts, les gazons verts, les mousses vertes; le vert serpente dans les troncs, les tiges non mûres sont vertes; le vert est le fond de la nature, parce que le vert se marie facilement à tous les autres tons. (*OC*, 2: 422)

The speaker emerges in the accusative as green continues to be glorified. Red emerges and breaks into song: "What strikes me first of all is that everywhere . . . red sings the glory of green" (48). The "me" is drawn into relief as the language of the text becomes metaphoric, and both red and narration become the lyric language of song: "Ce qui me frappe d'abord, c'est que partout . . . le rouge chante la gloire du vert" (*OC*, 2: 422) ("What strikes me first of all is that everywhere . . . red sings the glory of green") (48). The text continues to describe a sort of chiaroscuro of reflecting and correspondent images prefiguring the poetic technique of the symbol, which will later also be confirmed in the Wagnerian leitmotif.

> Les arbres, les rocher, les granits se mirent . . . et déposent leurs *reflets* . . . ceux-ci se renvoient leur reflets . . . de rouges fanfares s'élancent de tous côtés; une sanglante harmonie éclate à l'horizon, et le vert s'empourpre richement." (*OC*, 2: 423)

> The sap rises and there is a flowering [s'épanouir] of *mixed tones*; trees, rocks and granite boulders gaze at themselves in the water and cast their reflections upon them . . . Some colours cast back their reflections upon one another . . . fanfares of red surge forth on all sides; a harmony of blood flares up at the horizon, and green turns richly crimson. (49)

The green of verse asserts itself through this image prefiguring the Delacroix strophe of "Les Phares." The enunciating voice lays down verse, or green, from the very first word of the text: *supposons*, let us suppose or place down. The ambiguous green verse becomes the common place of synaesthetic articulation, moving through the irreducible interactions of color masses to resound in the red and bloody fanfare. Music emanates from the interaction of colors. The harmony articulated, however, preserves the differences out of which it is constituted: red and green are maintained.

The same relationships of mirroring—reflecting, responding, and resounding—take place among colors and natural objects that we saw extending in the long echoes of the poem "Correspondances." Color is the irreducible place of this interaction. Baudelaire concludes,

> Symphonie du jour . . . cette succession de mélodies, la variété sort de l'infini, cet hymne s'appelle la couleur. On trouve dans la couleur l'harmonie, la mélodie et le contrepoint." (*OC*, 2: 423)

> This great symphony of the day, which is an eternal variation of the symphony of yesterday, this succession of melodies whose variety ever issues from the infinite, this complex harmony is called *colour*. (49)

Music articulates time on the ground of color. Poetry (*vers*), color, and music are put into correspondence. The *Salon* itself is a place of synaesthesia.[19] In the same short essay, Baudelaire famously quotes E. T. A. Hoffmann to spell out what is usually referred to as the doctrine of correspondence: "It is not only in dreams, or in that mild delirium which precedes sleep, but it is even awakened when I hear music—that perception of an analogy and an intimate connexion between colours, sounds and perfumes. . . . The smell of red and brown marigolds above all produces a magical effect of my being. It makes me fall into a deep reverie, in which I seem to hear the solemn, deep tones of the oboe in the distance" (51). Baudelaire's quotation here prefigures its own later echo in "Correspondences," invoking the alignment of "colours, sounds and perfumes," and the softness of the oboe.

The next essay in the 1846 *Salon* is a text on Delacroix. Like Hugo, Delacroix crosses the arts. The two are set up in a transmedial chiasmus: "M. Victor Hugo est devenu un peintre en poésie; Delacroix . . . est souvent . . . un poète en peinture" (*OC*, 2: 432) ("M. Victor Hugo has become a painter in poetry; Delacroix . . . is often . . . a poet in painting") (57). Like Hugo, Delacroix has an exceptional relationship to the dictionary: "Pour E. Delacroix . . . la nature est un vaste dictionnaire . . ." ("For E. Delacroix . . . nature is a vast dictionary").

In another essay, a similar figure describes Hugo's ability to dip into the bottomless well of universal analogy, or correspondence. What joins and also distinguishes Hugo and Delacroix here is their ability to deploy available elements in original or new ways; their excellence resides precisely in the syntactical singularity of concrete utterances or usages, in the placed exposure of elements to one another (cf. 627).[20] Like green and red, Hugo and Delacroix are exposed to each other in the exterior of their extension, as signifiers spread out on a page, not as conscious or psychological subjects in communion. Subjects, that is, proper names, are joined in lines—*vers*—just as colors and sounds are juxtaposed in their reverse—that is, *rêves*, dreams, extended into reveries, the medium of synaesthesia in Baudelaire's quote from Hoffmann (425–26).

In the waking dream of green, *vert*, or *vers* or verse, waves break on the exposed edge of singularities. These encounters take place in the vague places—the *lieux vagues*—of others, in the murmuring fanfare of repeated speech and commingling voices. "Edgar Poe dit, je ne sais plus où" ("Edgar Poe speaks, I'm not sure where"), writes Baudelaire, "of the expansive nature of opium" (*OC* 2: 596). Baudelaire mingles, shares, or divides his own voice with Poe, as well as Hoffmann, in articulating synaesthesia, asking, "Who has not known those miraculous moments . . . when the senses are keenest . . . when sounds chime like music, when colours speak, and scents tell of whole worlds of ideas?" (143).

Baudelaire's repetitions and citations of others syncopate and parcel out his own voice. Similarly, his own voice resounds in the association of Delacroix and Weber first articulated in the *Salon* of 1846, in which he writes: "This lofty and serious melancholy of his shines with a gloomy brilliance, even in his colour, which is broad, simple and abundant in harmonious masses, like that of all the great colourists; and yet it is as plaintive and deep-toned as a melody of Weber" (66/440). As we have seen, the comparison is taken up again in "Beacon Lights" ("Les Phares"); the "fanfare" repeats the title of the poem as it weaves repeated terms across the years.

Baudelaire makes another anonymous appearance in the essay on Delacroix in the *Exposition Universelle* of 1855. Here he describes the material resilience of color while drawing attention to the hidden power of rhetoric.

> Il semble que cette couleur, qu'on me pardonne ces subterfuges de langage pour exprimer des idées fort delicates, pense par elle-même, indépendamment des objets qu'elle habille. (*CO*, 2: 595)

> If the reader will pardon me a stratagem of language in order to express an idea of some subtlety, it seems to me that M. Delacroix's colour *thinks on its own*, independently of the objects which it clothes. (141)

The singularity of Baudelaire's own quatrain is then invoked to expand further on the qualities of Delacroix' painting.

> Un poète a essayé d'exprimer ces sensations subtiles dans des vers don't la sincérité peut faire passer la bizarrerie.

> A poet has attempted to express these subtle sensations in some lines whose sincerity must excuse their singularity [*bizarrerie*].

Then follows the quatrain on Delacroix later included in "Les Phares." (The same technique, but with signature, is used in Baudelaire's essay on Wagner, where he cites "Correspondances.") The community of artists, then, like the synaesthesia of the senses, emerges through the murmuring repetition of letters, and holds open the common place—the green ground or verse base, the inverted dream—the reverse, or *rêve-vers* (dream-verse).

Repetitions, citations, syncopations, sobs, waves, tremors, quaking, laughter: these all structure the spasmodic dislocation of the other synaesthesia. A network expands through Baudelaire's writing that sets the senses, the arts, and singular names into an interplay and circulation that can be understood as a common place, or a kind of community. The differences of senses, of media, and of singular names persist in multiple rhythms and interrelations that at times collide or coincide, but do not fall into a harmony. The syncopated rhythm of a line of verse, the harmonious or bloody interactions of red and green, the evanescent fanfare of the interweaving of the arts: these criss-cross and intersect one another, but do not fall into a unifying beat. Beat itself, whether poetic or musical, remains one element among many.

The deorganizing of the senses through this inverse reading of synaesthesia comes into view in Gilles Deleuze's notion of the body without organs. In *The Logic of Sensation*, Deleuze suggests a community of arts that cuts across their difference: "the question concerning the separation of the arts, their respective autonomy, and their possible hierarchy loses all importance. For there is a community of the arts, a common problem. In art, and in painting as in music, it is not a matter of reproducing or inventing forms, but of capturing forces" (48). He thus suggests a unity of Rhythm, which he goes so far as to write with a capital letter, as the unity that manifests itself in any individual art—even though rhythm cannot really have an identity of its own, since its very definition is to exceed the limits of the body as a unifying figure ("We can seek the unity of rhythm only at the point where rhythm itself plunges into chaos, into the night, at the point where the differences of level are perpetually and violently mixed" [39]). Jean-Luc Nancy, in contrast, stresses the heterogeneity of elements that prevents their gathering into a single sense. This heterogeneity, for Nancy, culminates in the sense of touch. He writes: "Synesthetic synergy consists in nothing other than the auto-heterology of touch. . . . But what does art do if not finally touch upon and touch by means of the principal heterogeneity of 'sensing'? In this heterogeneity in principle that resolves itself into a heterogeneity *of the* principle, art touches on the sense of touch itself: in other words, it touches at once on the 'self-touching' inherent in touch and on the 'interruption' that is no less inherent in it" (*The Muses* 17–18). Baudelaire, too, endorses this persistence through touching of differences that form a synaesthetic chain in the prose world of criticism, a prose forest that brings together the many arts and works in their singularity. All the arts, Baudelaire writes, are "the expression of the beautiful through the feeling, the passion and the dreams of each one—that is to say a variety within a unity, or the various faces of the absolute—so criticism touches at every moment upon metaphysics" (*Art in Paris* 45, translation emended) ("sont toujours le beau exprimé par le sentiment, la passion et la rêverie de chacun, c'est-à-dire la variété dans l'unité, ou les faces diverses de l'absolu,— la critique touche à chaque instant à la métaphysique") (*OC*, 2: 419).

Chapter 4

Nietzsche, Wagner, and "Demonic Communicability"

The story of Nietzsche and Wagner is well known. It is a story of the older master and the young academic who lent him prestige, of the "Tribschen Idyll": the time during which Nietzsche visited the Wagners from his nearby home in Basel. The usual story tends to follow Nietzsche's own account and see his involvement with Wagner as a kind of sickness or failing that he himself soon overcame. One recent critic argues that Nietzsche was, in fact, only a Wagnerian for a mere year and a half. The reception tends to minimize Nietzsche's youthful error and focus instead on his self-correction; or, conversely, to defend Wagner and ascribe Nietzsche's turn to his own personality flukes. But their break is something more than this; as Avital Ronell writes in *The Test Drive*, "Nietzsche loved Wagner. . . . What led him to break the friendship of ten years was not intersubjective but ethical. It was not a whim, a mood, an episode, a sense of harm or an account of the other's wrong doing that instantiated the break" (285). Here, I would like to try to understand Nietzsche's love for Wagner and his turn away from him not in terms of the psychology of the two men, but rather in terms of the logic of mimesis that subtends them both. The reversibility of this logic surfaces in a peculiar quality Nietzsche attributes to Wagner: "dämonische Mittheilbarkeit," that is, demonic communicability or impartability.

I propose that we think of Wagner not as a person, but as a kind of language. In the opening of the fourth *Untimely Meditation*, Nietzsche introduces Wagner as a kind of linguistic event that is essentially relational: "Damit ein Ereignis Grösse habe, muss zweierlei zusammenkommen: der grosse Sinn Derer, die es vollbringen und der grosse Sinn Derer, die es erleben" (*KSA*, 1: 431) ("For an event to possess greatness two things must come together: greatness of spirit in those who accomplish it and greatness of spirit in those who experience it") (*UM*, 197). There must be a "Sich-entsprechen von That und Empfänglichkeit . . . Der, welcher geben will, muss zusehen, dass er die Nehmer findet, die dem Sinne seiner Gabe genugthun" (*KSA*, 1: 431) ("correspondence between deed and receptivity; and he who gives must see to it that he finds recipients adequate to the meaning of his gift") (197). Neither position has value or effectiveness individually; only in this correspondence between giving and taking can exchange, or communication, take place. This contrasts with the general condition of language in Wagner's historical time. Nietzsche suggests, "überall ist hier die Sprache erkrant" (455) ("everywhere *language* is sick") (214). This sickness consists in the orientation of language solely toward "das Reich des Gedankens" ("the realm of thought") at the expense of feeling or *Empfindung*. With the advance of civilization, language has become exhausted, "so dass sie nicht mehr zu leisten vermag, wessentwegen sie allein da ist: um über die einfachsten Lebensnöthen die Leidenden miteinander zu verständigen. Der Mensch kann sich in seiner Noth vermöge der Sprache nicht mehr zu erkennen geben, also sich nicht wahrhaft mittheilien" (1: 455) ("so that it is now no longer capable of performing that function for the sake of which alone it exists: to enable suffering mankind to come to an understanding with one another over the simplest needs of life. Man can no longer express his needs and distress by means of language, thus he can no longer really communicate [sich mittheilen] at all") (214). Wagner is an exception to this decayed language and inability to communicate. In him, Ur-nature "kann nicht anders als mittheilen, Jedermann soll an ihrem Werke mitwirken, sie geizt nicht mit ihren Gaben" (465) ("can do nothing other than communicate, everyone is to collaborate in its work, it is not niggardly with its gifts") (222).

Through Wagner's work, Nietzsche writes, music speaks as the language of the soul that seeks a body for itself, thus putting music and "gymnastic" or gesture into a form or *Gestalt*. The audience participates by receiving this new language or this language of the new.

> Helft mir, so ruft er allen zu, die hören können, helft mir jene Cultur zu entdecken, von der meine Musik als die wiedergefundene Sprache der richtigen Empfindung wahrsagt, denkt darüber nach, das die Seele der Musik sich jetzt einen Leib gestalten will, dass sie durch euch alle hindurch zur Sichtbarkeit in Bewegung, That, Einrichtung und Sitte ihren Weg sucht! (1: 458).

> Help me, he cries to all who can hear, help me to discover that culture whose existence my music, as the rediscovered language of true feeling, prophesies; reflect that the soul of music now wants to create for itself a body, that it seeks its path through all of you to visibility in movement, deed, structure and morality! (217).

The question of realization, or the becoming physical/Gestalt of music, is the question of the relation between Music and life, compared to the relation between two languages: "Das Verhältnis zwischen Musik und Leben ist nicht nur das einer Art Sprache zu einer anderen Art Sprache, es ist auch das Verhältniss der vollkommenen Hörwelt zu der gesammten Schauwelt" (1: 456) ("The relation between music and life is not only that of one kind of language to another kind of language, it is also the relationship between the perfect world of sound and the totality of the world of sight") (215). The giving of plasticity is equated with the translation between one language and another. Synaesthesia is enacted as a translation between sound and vision, between music and life.

This translatability, for Wagner, is originally figured as the coming forth of the God Apollo in Greek tragedy, which Wagner understood to be the first *Gesamtkunstwerk*. In Greek tragedy, according to Wagner, the god himself becomes present and real. With this embodiment—a unity of the earthly and the divine, of the immanent and the transcendent—the difference between the senses disappears along with the dichotomy between spectacle and audience. Generality and individual become reciprocally interchangeable. "In der Tragödie," writes Wagner,

> fand er [the Greek] sich ja selbst wieder . . . vereinigt mit den edelsten Teilen des Gesamtwesens der ganzen Nation; aus sich selbst . . . sprach er sich durch das tragische Kunstwerk das Orakel der Pythia . . . herrlicher, göttlicher Mensch, er in der Allgemeinheit, die Allgemeinheit in ihm. (*DS*, 5: 277)

> For in the tragedy he found himself again . . . found the noblest part of his own nature united with the noblest characteristics of the whole nation; and from his inmost soul . . . proclaimed the Pythian oracle. At once both God and Priest, glorious godlike man, one with the Universal, the Universal summed up in him.[1]

The Greek tragedy, as the original *Gesamtkunstwerk*, is dependent on a form of community in which individual and universal, part and whole, are organically intertwined, a thoroughly integrated organic community. The communal *Gesamtkunstwerk* of the Greeks depends first of all on this literalization of Apollo, a kind of personification in which he steps forth onto the stage: "Das war das griechische Kunstwerk, das der zu wirklicher, lebendiger Kunst gewordene Apollon,—das war das griechische Volk in seiner höchsten Wahrheit und Schönheit" (5: 276) ("Such was the Grecian work of art; such their God Apollo, incarnated in actual, living art; such was the Grecian people in its highest truth and beauty") (33).

Personification here functions as the embodiment, the making real and individual, of a transcendent general content. In the modern music drama, the creative artist—that is, Wagner himself—takes the place of Apollo and incarnates himself in the actor, the presenting artist. The displacement of the artist onto the actor is then doubled in the relationship between the actor and the hero he represents. The figure of the artist/hero combines all the art forms while it also closes the gap between art and life, between actor (*Darsteller*) and poet (*Dichter*). This unification takes place in and as the event of communication (*Mitteilung*). The artist thus imparts or divides himself (in Wagner, this figure is masculine) in solidifying the commonality or community.

> Als Tänzer, Tonkünstler und Dichter ist er aber eines und dasselbe, nichts anderes als darstellender, künstlerischer Mensch, der sich nach der höchsten Fülle seiner Fähigkeiten an die höchste Empfängniskraft mitteilt. In ihm, dem unmittelbaren Darsteller, vereinigen sich die drei Schwesterkünste zu einer gemeinsame Wirksamkeit. . . . Indem sie gemeinsam wirken, gewinnt jede von ihnen das Vermögen, gerade das sein und leisten zu können, was sie ihrem eignetümlichsten Wesen nach zu sein und zu leisten verlangen. Dadurch, daß jede da, wo ihr Vermögen endet, in die andere, von da ab vermögende, aufgehen kann, bewahrte sich rein, frei und selbständig als das, was sie ist. (6: 133–34)

> But as dancer, tone-artist, and poet, he still is one and the same thing: nothing other than *executant, artistic Man, who, in the fullest measure of his faculties, imparts himself to the highest expression of receptive power*. It is in him, the immediate executant, that the three sister-arts unite their forces in one collective operation. . . . By working in common, each one of them attains the power to be and do the very thing which, of her own and

inmost essence, she longs to do and be. Hereby: that each, where her own power ends, can be absorbed within the other, whose power commences where hers ends,—she maintains her own purity and freedom, her independence as that which she is. (189)

The individual art becomes most itself in ceasing to be, in joining forces and merging with a totality. The singular figure, in exposing itself through communication, becomes generic or general (*Mensch*). This transition is likewise envisioned as a ceasing to be, or death.

Der Dichter aber wird wahrhaft erst Mensch durch sein Übergehen in das Fleisch und Blut des Darstellers; . . . so wird diese Absicht aus seinem Wollen zum Können erst dadurch, daß eben dieses dichterische Wollen im Können der Darstellung untergeht. (6: 134)

While the *Poet* first becomes a Man through his translation to the flesh and blood of the *Performer* . . . this purpose is first changed from "will" to "can" *by the poet's Will descending to the actor's Can.* (190)

Presentation (*Darstellung*) is thus essential to the fulfillment and realization of the artist/subject.[2] The turn into the flesh and blood of the act of performance is aligned with the event of communication (*Mitteilung*); thus as the agent is partitioned between self and other, he communicates himself to others and becomes general.

Das notwendigste und stärkste Bedürfnis des vollkommenen künstlerischen Menschen ist aber, sich selbst, in der höchsten Fülle seines Wesens, der vollsten Gemeinsamkeit mitzuteilen. . . . In Drama erweitert er ein besonderes Wesen durch Darstellung einer individuellen Persönlichkeit, die er nicht selbst ist, zum allgemein menschlichen Wesen. (6: 137)

The most imperious and strongest need of full-fledged artist-man, however, is to impart himself in highest compass of his being to the fullest expression of Community. . . . In Drama he broadens out his own particular being, by the portrayal of an individual personality not his own, to a universally human being. (193)

The series of displacements Wagner envisions answers to what Jean-Luc Nancy has analyzed as the "magnetic chain of enthusiasm" set forth in Plato's *Ion*. The "partage des voix" in his work of that name points to the coexistence of receptivity and spontaneity, of passion and action, in the wake of the "theia moira," or the divine partitioning, that gives rise to communicative community. But this possibility, for Nancy, begins with the lack of proper qualities required of the poet, thus is grounded in a nonidentity and singularity.

For Wagner, the figure of the poet only becomes himself in becoming another (presentation), in the dissimulation of the actor. The principle of identity is undermined, therefore, even as it is asserted. As it shifts from poet to performer (*Darsteller*), one might be tempted to relocate identity in the position of the actor; but that position is also immediately displaced onto that of the hero. In the hero, the individual fully sacrifices himself to the general in a necessary death. The frame of representation, drama, lends necessity to an event that, in life, would still be particular, random or chance (6: 142). The ordering of the plot renders events necessary. In ordering the acts and deeds onstage, the actor (*Darsteller*) lends necessity to the chance events of the life of the (represented) hero. "Der Darsteller wird in seinem Drange nach künstlerischer Reproduktion der Handlung somit Dichter" (144) ("In his stress for artistic reproduction of the Action, the performer thus becomes a poet") (200).

The double valence of the word *Handlung*—both plot and act or action—allows for the interchangeability of hero and actor through which the actor becomes the ordering poet and the hero takes up the position of the actor. That is, the relation between poet and actor is doubled by that between the actor and his hero. The *Dichter* becomes *Darsteller*, and the *Darsteller* becomes the *Dichter*.

For the early Nietzsche, this slippage of the subject devolves outward to encompass the spectator as well. He attributes this self-alienation or divisiveness to what he calls Wagner's fundamental translatability and/or communicability: "dämonische Uebertragbarkeit" and "dämonische Mittheilbarkeit"[3] ("demonic transmissibility" and "demonic communicability"[4]). By virtue of this quality, the artist divides and parcels himself out (*teilt*) in communicating; the spectator participates (*nimmt teil*) through the same *Mittheilung* or event of divisive communication. In the face of Wagner, Nietzsche writes in the fourth *Untimely Meditation*, the spectator feels himself alienated from his own essence; "Denn gerade mit diesem Gefühle nimmet er Theil an der gewaltigsten Lebensäusserung

Wagner's, dem Mittelpuncte seiner Kraft, jener dämonische Uebertragbarkeit und Selbstentäusserung seiner Natur, welche sich Anderen ebenso mittheilen kann, als sie andere Wesen sich selber mittheilt und im Hingeben und Annehmen ihre Grösse hat. Indem der Betrachtende scheinbar der aus- und überströmenden Natur Wagner's unterliegt, hat er an ihrer Kraft selber Antheil genommen" (*KSA*, 1: 466) ("For it is with precisely this feeling that he participates in Wagner's mightiest accomplishment, the central point of his power, the demonic *transmissibility* and self-relinquishment of his nature, with which others are able to communicate just as readily as it communicates with other natures, and whose greatness consists in its capacity both to surrender and to receive. By apparently succumbing to Wagner's overflowing nature, he who reflects upon it has in fact participated in its energy") (222–23).

This sympathetic partitioning communication coincides with synaesthesia.

> In Wagner will alles Sichtbare der Welt zum Hörbaren sich vertiefen und verinnerlichen . . . in Wagner will ebenso alles Hörbare der Welt auch als Erscheinung für das Auge an's Licht hinaus und hinauf, will gleichsam Leiblichkeit gewinnen. (*KSA*, 1: 467)

> In Wagner all that is visible in the world wants to become more profound and more intense by becoming audible . . . and . . . all that is audible in the world likewise wants to emerge into the light and also become a phenomenon for the eye; . . . it wants as it were to acquire corporality. (223)

The combining of the visual and the audible (synaesthesia) coincides with the passage between inside and outside figured as expression. "Dies Alles ist das Wesen des dithyrambischen Dramatikers, diesen Begriff so voll genommen, das er zugleich den Schauspieler, Dichter, Musiker umfasst" (*KSA*, 1: 467) ("All this constitutes the essence of the *dithyrambic dramatist*, this concept extended to embrace at once the actor, poet and composer") (223).

The reception of Wagner's work causes the spectator to deeply question himself about his own reason for being, to pose this question which, because it has no answer, results in a kind of self-alienation. Wagner's nature is an infinitely giving source that transfers and translates itself unto its recipients; communication and self-alienation/self-expression overlap so that self-division becomes participation in an other. This sense of artistic communication as a simultaneous sharing and partitioning—*Mittheilung*—should be distinguished from an instrumental sense of language that would convey a message or information. Thus Wagner's greatness, for Nietzsche, cannot be rendered in any kind of a meaning, but rather is located in the potential for translating, sharing partitioning that describes it in general terms.

> So muss die Grösse Wagners, des Künstlers, gerade in jener dämonische Mittheilbarkeit seiner Natur bestehen, welche gleichsam in allen Sprachen von sich redet und das innere, eigenste Erlebniss mit der höchsten Deutlichkeit erkennen lässt. (*KSA*, 1: 485)

> Wagner's greatness as an artist must consist in precisely that demonic *communicability* of his nature, which as it were speaks of itself in every language and makes known its inner, most personal experience with the extremist clarity. (236)

The model of *Mittheilung* as a kind of communication overlaps with the mimetic model of representation implied in Wagner's theory of the *Gesamtkunstwerk*. As the artist parcels himself out, the receiver experience self-alienation in participating in the communication or representation he receives. The modeling of Apollo in Greek tragedy follows a Platonic logic of mimetic embodiment that unifies singular and idea in what Nietzsche calls "the example" or the individual. This is why in his later texts he quotes Plato on the mimetic artist to criticize Wagner. It constitutes simultaneously a self-externalization or alienation (*Selbstentäusserung*) that structures communication (*Mittheilung*). The universal dithyrambic artist combines the various roles, as we have seen outlined in Wagner's own writings. The overlap between actor and poet, *Schauspieler* und *Dichter*, is especially important here as it enacts the slippage outlined above.

The reading of Wagner and Nietzsche together here sheds a somewhat different light on Nietzsche's later argument against Wagner that he is really not a musician, but an actor. In *Der Fall Wagner*, *The Case of Wagner*, Nietzsche declares that the slippage from musician to actor is an instance of decay, not of fulfillment.

> Der letztere, ein Charakter-Verfall, käme vielleicht mit dieser Formel zu einem vorläufigen Ausdruck: der Musiker wird jetzt

zum Schauspieler, seine Kunst entwickelt sich immer mehr als ein Talent zu lügen. (*KSA*, 6: 26)

The latter, the decay of character, could perhaps find preliminary expression in this formula: the musician now becomes an actor, his art develops more and more as a talent to *lie*. (*CW*, in *The Birth of Tragedy and the Case of Wagner*, 169)

The actor both expresses and dissimulates, the one function implicated in the other.

The *Mitteilbarkeit* the early Nietzsche attributes to Wagner, I would like to suggest, is reversible. It is both a praiseworthy quality of Wagner, solidifying the subject in unifying poet, actor, and composer; and a negative capacity for infinite displacement of the subject position, and thus a dissimulating quality. The two-sided nature of this quality is what makes it "demonic." Nietzsche is thus attracted and repelled by the very same quality. Thus the problem of this demonic communicability would be integral to Nietzsche's "turn" regarding Wagner.[5] This turn is the turn or reversal of mimesis itself. Samuel Weber translates the term "*Mitteilbarkeit*" as "impartability" in his book *Benjamin's -abilities*, especially in chapter 4, "Impart-ability: Language as Medium." Here Weber traces Benjamin's use of the term "*Mitteilbarkeit*" to describe the mediacy of language. Thus conceived, "language still retains one decisive aspect of the means, which is that it is not self-contained, complete, perfect, or perfectible. It is simply *there*, but as something that splits off from itself, takes leave of itself, *parts with* what it was to become something else, to be transposed, transmitted, or translated into something else" (42). The reversibility of *Mitteilbarkeit* thus would point always to its decentering force rather than the stabilization of identity at which it was at first aimed.

Wagnerian *Mittheilbarkeit* is grounded in a suprapersonal "nature" that appears through Wagner's works, just as his vision of Greek tragedy was grounded in the divinity. Nature must be given a language: "Von Wagner . . . wäre im allgemein zu sagen, dass er Allem in der Natur, was bis jetzt nicht reden wollte, eine Sprache gegeben hat: er glaubt nicht daran, dass es etwas Stummes geben müsse" (*KSA*, 1: 491) ("Of Wagner . . . it can be said in general that he has bestowed a language upon everything in nature which has hitherto not wanted to *speak*: he does not believe that anything is obliged to be dumb") (*UM*, 240). Wagner translates nature into music, word, and gesture; these, in turn, are the appearances (*Erscheinung*) of an interior. This inner/outer structure is repeated in the representing persons onstage, who in turn transfer an effect (*Wirkung*) to the audience (488). The effect on the spectator is supposed to be the direct transference (*Übertragung*) of an interior. Appearance is externalization and utterance, that is, *Entäusserung*. Wagner, Nietzsche writes, surprises the deepest inner secrets of nature—that which has no language of its own—and brings it to appearance.

> Das bisher Unsichtbare, Innere rettet sich in die Sphäre des Sichtbaren und wird Erscheinung; das bisher nur Sichtbare flieht in das dunkle Meer des Tönenden: so enthüllt die Natur, indem sie sich verstecken will, das Wesen ihrer Gegensätze. (471)

> What has hitherto been invisible and inward escapes into the sphere of the visible and becomes appearance; what was hitherto only visible flees into the dark ocean of the audible: *thus by seeking to hide herself, nature reveals the character of her antitheses.* (*UM*, 226)

In his essay "Diderot: Paradox and Mimesis," Philippe Lacoue-Labarthe outlines this as the way in which mimesis supplements nature, revealing the hidden "gift of nothing" that underlies it. Once this gift passes over into the given, or the potentiality of *Mittheilbarkeit* passes into the fact of a *Mittheilung*, these have an independent existence that surpasses the original they allow to come into appearance. The excess of appearance, following a Platonic logic, is of course the simulacrum, or what Nietzsche calls *Schein* or *Anschein*. The fall from *Erscheinung* to *Schein* is allied with Nietzsche's understanding of decadence and goes back to the decayed state of language with which I began: "Die Erscheinung des modernen Menschen ist ganz und gar Schein geworden; er wird in dem, was er jetzt vorstellt, nicht selber sichtbar, viel eher versteckt" (*KSA*, 1: 457) ("The phenomenon of modern man has become wholly appearance; he is not visible in what he represents but rather concealed by it") (216).

Nietzsche's critique of Wagner is based in his claim that Wagner no longer externalizes or expresses, but merely manufactures works to produce effects. The *Mittheilung* thus is no longer grounded either in Nature or in a god. The ungrounding of mimesis lets loose all the negativity of mere "effects" without sufficient cause. Stripped of *Geist* or *Seele*, spirit or soul, the material aspects of the work effect the spectator physiologically:

"Klang, Bewegung, Farbe, kurz die Sinnlichkeit der Musik . . . er will die Wirkung, nichts als die Wirkung" (*KSA*, 6: 31) ("sound, movement, color, in brief the sensuousness of music . . . what he wants is effect, nothing but effect") (173). Wagner works directly on his nerves: or rather Hers. This position of passivity in relation to mimesis, as Lacoue-Labarthe shows, is traditionally associated with the feminine, and in Nietzsche too. Because of the participation of the audience in the work, Nietzsche derisively calls them "Wagnerianer," the epitome of which is really the "Wagnerianerin." Wagnerian art becomes a system of seduction and persuasion that understands itself as an instrumental language. Wagner made of music "eine Theater-Rhetorik, ein Mittel des Ausdrucks, der Gebärden-Verstärkung, der Suggestion . . . er hat das Sprachvermögen der Musik in's Unermessliche vermehrt . . . Sprache [as] Werkzeug" (*KSA*, 6: 30) ("theatrical rhetoric, a means of expression, of underscoring gestures, of suggestion . . . *he has increased music's capacity for language to the point of making it immeasurable*") (172–73). Wagner becomes the master of the art of presentation, without relation to a hidden origin, exemplified by the actor or the bad virtuoso (38).

Critics and historians tend to locate Nietzsche's turn away from Wagner in his "disappointment with the Bayreuth project" in the 1870s.[6] And this is no surprise, since Bayreuth is in a way the ultimate incorporation of an idea meant to create a certain effect, and indeed the effect of illusion. In his speech given at the laying of the foundation stone of the *Festspielhaus* in Bayreuth, Wagner explicitly states that the theater will be the embodiment of his thought and that the name itself stands for a whole constellation of relations and meanings. The architectural arrangement of Bayreuth effects a displacement of the spectator that inaugurates the effect of the music and the drama. As is well known, Wagner instituted many innovations in the theater built at Bayreuth, among them: the concealment of the orchestra in the orchestra pit; the elimination of boxes on the sides of the theater; and a double proscenium that increased perspectival illusion and made the actors appear to be larger than life.

In Bayreuth, the future is now. Wagner writes,

> Soll diese Wirkung bereits rein und vollkommen sein, so wird nun der geheimnisvolle Eintritt der Musik Sie auf die Enthüllung und deutliche Vorführung von scenischen Bildern vorbereiten, welche, wie sie aus einer idealen Traumwelt vor Ihnen sich darzustellen scheinen, die ganze Wirklichkeit der sinnovllsten Täuschung einer edlen Kunst vor Ihnen kundgeben sollen. Hier darf nichts

> mehr in blossen Andeutungen eben nur provisorisch zu Ihnen sprechen; so weit das künstlerische Vermögen der Gegenwart reicht, soll Ihnen im szenischen, wie im mimischen Spiele das Vollendete geboten werden. (*DS*, 10: 25)

> Should this effect already be pure and complete, then the mysterious entry of the music will prepare you for the revealing and clear presentation of scenic images. These, which seem to present themselves in front of you from out of an ideal dream world, should announce to you the whole reality of the most meaningful illusion of a noble art. Here, nothing more will speak to you in mere suggestions as if only provisionally; as far as the artistic capacity of the present reaches, what is complete and perfected will be offered to you in the scenic and in the mimetic play. (My translation)

The physical building becomes the determining ground of the illusory effect of the music drama, rather than the interiority of the composer's nature. Bayreuth is an inverted world that allows Nietzsche to say: "was als wahr wirken soll, darf nicht wahr sein. . . . Wagner's Musik ist niemals wahr" (31) ("What is meant to have the effect of truth must not be true. . . . Wagner's music is never true") (173). This, Nietzsche elucidates, is the defining psychology of the mimetic actor.

Mitteilbarkeit, or impartability,[7] draws Wagnerism into the realm of the "paradox of the actor" outlined already by Diderot.[8] It should be remembered, too, that "allgemeine Mitteilbarkeit" is what Kant names the quality of aesthetic experience prior to the sensation of pleasure in an object.[9] Synaesthesia helps constitute this *Mitteilbarkeit*, offering up the elements of accumulation and the independent members of a community, whether they be senses, sense data, or individual artists.

Chapter 5

The Unworking of Synaesthesia in Joris-Karl Huysmans's *À Rebours*

In Wagner's aesthetics, and what is often called the mystical conception of synaesthesia, the boundaries between the arts, and in fact the individual arts themselves, dissolve for the sake of a higher concept: that of Art in general. Wagner articulates this process of sublation as follows:

> Nur die Kunst, die dieser Allfähigkeit des Menschen entspricht, ist somit *frei*, nicht die Kunst*art*, die nur von einer einzelnen menschlichen Fähigkeit herrührt. Tanzkunst, Tonkunst und Dichtkunst sind vereinzelt jede beschränkt; in der Berührung ihrer Schranken fühlt jede sich unfrei, sobald sie an ihrem Grenzpunkte nicht der anderen entsprechenden Kunstart in unbedingt anerkennender Liebe die Hand reicht. Schon das erfassen dieser Hand hebt sie über die Schranke hinweg; die vollständige Umschlingen, das vollständige Aufgehen in der Schwester, d.h. das vollständige Aufgehen ihrer selbst jenseits der gestellten Schranke, läßt aber die Schranke ebenfalls vollständig fallen; und sind alle Schranken in dieser Weise gefallen, so sind weder die Kunstarten, noch aber auch eben diese Schranken mehr vorhanden, sondern nur die *Kunst*, die gemeinsame, unbeschränkte Kunst selbst. (6: 38–39)

> The Arts of dance, of tone, of Poetry, are each confined within their several bounds [Beschränkungen]; in contact with these bounds each feels herself unfree, be it not that, across their

common boundary, she reaches out her hand to her neighbouring art in unrestrained acknowledgment of love. The very grasping of this hand lifts her above the barrier; her full embrace, her full absorption in her sister—i.e. her own complete ascension beyond the set-up barrier—casts down the fence itself. And when every barrier has thus fallen, then are there no more arts and no more boundaries, but only Art, the universal, undivided. (98)

For someone like Jean-Luc Nancy, in contrast, or Adorno ("Die Kunst und die Künste"), the specificity of the arts consists precisely in the preponderance of exteriority that resists such a sublation. Nancy writes in *Les Muses*: "In one way or another, art would thus be in default or in excess of its own concept . . . Art and the arts interbelong to each other in a tense, extended mode in exteriority, without any resolution in interiority" (4). Dwelling in exteriority, synaesthesia coarticulates the senses and the arts without unifying them; dissolving boundaries, it abides in the particular senses and arts it combines. In this sense, synaesthesia is an unworking of aesthetic totality, a dissolution of wholeness and transcendence that yet preserves and extends differences. The unworking of synaesthesia I propose to trace out in Joris-Karl Huysmans's decadent novel, *À Rebours* (1884), usually translated as *Against Nature*, connects the senses and the arts without doing away with differences. Moments of apparent unification alternate with processes of dispersion and dissemination. The vocabularies of individual arts and senses are maintained as they are enlisted to articulate other arts and senses and to overcome differences. Metonymy is the dominant figure through which the senses and the arts are concatenated.

For Max Nordau, author of the infamous work *Degeneration* (1892), synaesthesia precisely does away with differences to regress to a state of physiological nondifferentiation. He writes,

> It is evidence of diseased and debilitated brain-activity, if consciousness relinquishes the advantages of the differentiated perceptions of phenomena, and carelessly confounds the reports conveyed by the particular senses. It is a retrogression to the very beginning of organic development. It is a descent from the height of human perfection to the low level of the mollusk. To raise the combination, transposition and confusion of the perceptions to the rank of a principle of art, to see futurity in this principle, is to designate as progress the return from the consciousness of man to that of the oyster. (*Degeneration*, 142)

But as I show in what follows, the synaesthetic networks of *À Rebours* maintain differentiation among the arts and senses even in setting them up in a relay of sympathetic resemblances. Synaesthesia remains suspended between transcendent concept and mollusk.

Huysmans's novel opens as its protagonist, Floressas des Esseintes, moves to the outskirts of Paris, where he builds a home that will gratify all the senses. The narrative installs synaesthesia in the house, allowing des Esseintes to indulge all of his senses and connecting different modes of perception and genres of art. The house results from a kind of aesthetic technology, which attempts to build a stage for the scenes of sensible gratification and experience that constitute the novel. Des Esseintes constructs so-called eccentricities such as the famous taste-organ that both plays tones and emits liqueurs; fish-tank-like windows containing mechanical fish; and a bedroom decked out in watered silk and fine dark wood to simulate a barren monk's cell. He also collects art and books, carefully adding them to the décor.

Among the many items on display in des Esseintes's house are two paintings of Salome by Gustave Moreau. At first glance, Huysmans's treatments of them seem to follow the traditional structure of ekphrasis, the verbal representation of visual representation. Following Lessing, Murray Krieger's definition suggests that in ekphrasis, the temporal frame of discourse is interrupted by the spatial stillness of the image. Françoise Meltzer quotes Saintsbury on ekphrasis as follows: "a set description intended to bring person, place, picture, etc. vividly before the mind's eye" (21),[1] and Hagstrum, who "has called ekphrasis 'that special quality of giving voice and language to a mute art object'" (21). Taken together, these two definitions suggest that ekphrasis animates an image, making it vivid and present. Meltzer goes on to give the etymological sense of *ekphrazein*, meaning to "speak out," "to tell in full" (21). In Huysmans's descriptions of both *Salome Dancing before Herod* and the watercolor *L'Apparition*, the text shifts into the present tense as it comes to focus on the figure of Salome. The ekphrasis enacts prosopopoeia.[2]

While it is obvious how the visual and the textual work together, it is not usually noticed that smell also plays a large part in this process.[3] It is not so much that language makes an image "come alive." Instead, literature, painting, odor, and music cooperate to undo the frame around the painted image, letting it loose into the present tense of the narrative. Smell, in particular, plays an important role in this dissolution of diegetic boundaries. As is well known, Freud associates the sense of smell with sexuality, and points to it as a mode of sensation that was repressed and deprecated with the rise of man to an upright stance.[4] His view would accord well with Nordau's view of synaesthesia as evolutionary regression. For Huysmans, though, smell indicates an emanation, a movement upward and outward. Ultimately, smell will be directly compared to literature, its experience to that of language as something that can be manipulated and composed. The literary underpinnings of smell prevent it from returning to the state of the oyster deplored by Nordau.

The haze of incense is what first allows the vivification of the painting to occur.

> Autour de cette statue, immobile, figée dans une pose hiératique de dieu Hindou, des parfums brûlaient, dégorgeant des nuées de vapeurs que trouaient, de même que des yeux phosphorés de bêtes, les feux des piettes enchassées dans les parois du trône; puis la vapeur montait, se déroulait sous les arcades où la fumée bleue se mêlait à la poudre d'or des grands rayons de jour, tombés des dômes. (146)

> Round about this immobile, statuesque figure, frozen like some Hindu god in a hieratic pose, incense was burning, sending up clouds of vapour through which the fiery gems set in the sides of the throne gleamed like the phosphorescent eyes of wild animals. The clouds rose higher and higher, swirling under the arches of the roof, where the blue smoke mingled with the gold dust of the great beams of sunlight slanting down from the domes[5]). (51)

The jewels become animate as the smelly cloud moves upward and joins with the haze of sunlight. The present-tense Salome exceeds the material of paint. She emerges in a moment of synaesthesia that adjoins smell, music (sound) and vision, but leaves them distinct: "Dans l'odeur perverse des parfums, dans l'atmosphère surchauffée de cette église, Salomé . . . s'avance lentement sur les pointes, aux accords d'une guitare dont une femme accroupie pince les cordes" (146) ("Amid the heady odours of these perfumes, in the overheated atmosphere of the basilica, Salome slowly glides forward on the points of her toes . . . while a woman squatting on the floor strums the strings of the guitar") (51). Salome comes to life as the text moves into the present tense to narrate her movement; the scene of the painting and the scene of the narrative collapse. Des Esseintes's dreaming pose before the painting allows a dramatization of the figure of Salome, who now steps forth as if a living member of the narrative. The next paragraph slides, along with the now coming to life figure of Salome, into the present tense. It details the elements of the portrait of Salome in a heterogenous image that fragments the unity of the body. Body and clothing parts are intermingled without being unified; stones and jewels are sprinkled through the paragraph, attributed the powers of fire, life, and motion (cf. Meltzer).

> La face recueillie, solennelle, presque auguste, elle commence la lubrique danse qui doit réveiller les sens assoupis du vieil Hérode; ses seins ondulent . . . sur la moiteur de sa peau les diamants, attachés, scintillant; ses bracelets, ses ceintures, ses bagues, crachent des étincelles; sur sa robe triomphale, couture de perles, ramagée d'argent, lamée d'or, la cuirasse des orfèvreries dont chaque maille est une pierre, entre en combustion, croise des serpenteaux de feu, grouille sur la chair mate. (147)

> With a withdrawn, solemn, almost august expression on her face, she begins the lascivious dance which is to rouse the aged Herod's dormant senses; her breasts rise and fall . . . the strings of diamonds glitter against her moist flesh; her bracelets, her belts, her rings all spit out fiery sparks; and across her triumphal robe, sewn with pearls, patterned with silver, spangled with gold, the jeweled cuirass, of which every chain is a precious stone, seems to be ablaze with little snakes of fire, swarming over the mat-flesh. (51)

The stringing along of elements—breasts, flesh, rings, robe, pearls, and so on—intermix the body and its adornment without syntactical contouring or subordination. The mixing of elements recalls the stylistic heterogeneity of Moreau's painting, which joins a number of disparate cultural traditions in a heterogeneous stylistic and emblematic syncretism. Huysmans's prose begins to mirror Moreau's painterly technique. Peter Cooke, eminent scholar of Gustave Moreau, writes,

> As many critics of the time were quick to realize, in *Salome* Moreau has forged a chimerical synthesis of ancient civilisations. Indeed, wishing to create a "palais fantastique" this "craftsman assembler of dreams" has surpassed himself in his notoriously eclectic manipulation of iconographic sources, gathering together and fusing a collection of architectural and decorative elements drawn from reproductions of monuments as disparate as Hagia Sophia, the Alhambra of Granada, the Great Mosque of Cordoba and various medieval cathedrals. Motifs from Etruscan, Roman, Egyptian, Indian and Chinese art have also been identified.[6]

Though described as synthesis, there is here no sublation that renders a higher unity or concept. It is rather a juxtapositioning that preserves the particular entities, individually recognizable, out of which it is composed.[7]

As Meltzer and others point out, the figure of Salome is brought to life in Huysmans's text, but is at the same time turned into a strangely inanimate figure.[8] She is both brought to life and killed off in a single gesture: "Concentrée, les yeux fixes, semblable à une somnambule, elle ne voit ni le Tétrarque qui frémit, ni sa mère" (147) ("Her eyes fixed in the concentrated gaze of a sleepwalker, she sees neither the Tetrarch nor her mother . . .") (51). She is made into a symbol only to be transformed into an inanimate allegorical emblem. Fulfilling des Esseintes dream-image, "elle n'était plus seulement la baladine qui arrache à un vieillard, par une torsion corrompue de ses reins, un cri de désir et de rut . . . elle devenait, en quelque sorte, la déité symbolique de l'indestructible Luxure, la déesse de l'immortelle Hystérie, la Beauté maudite, élue entre toutes par la catalepsie qui lui raidit les chairs et lui durcit les muscles" (148–149) ("she was no longer just the dancing-girl who extorts a cry of lust and lechery from an old man by the lascivious movements of her loins. . . . she had become, as it were, the symbolic incarnation of undying Lust, the Goddess of immortal Hysteria, the accursed Beauty exalted above all other beauties by the catalepsy that hardens her flesh and steels her muscles") (53).

Emptied of an absent meaning toward which it points, the emblem freezes to a standstill. Cooke aligns this with the moment of stillness, of plastic beauty, that most of all characterizes the art of painting. He argues, "This is not a dance," but a painterly standstill. The function of the emblem of the lotus-blossom and its contiguity with the dead body replay the petrifaction and emptying out of Salome as a living figure.

> Des Esseintes cherchait le sens de cet emblème. . . . Peut-être s'était-il [Moreau] souvenu des rites de la vieille Egypte, des cérémonies sépulcrales de l'embaumement, alors que les chimistes et les prêtres étendent le cadavre de la morte sur un banc de jaspe, lui tirent avec des aiguilles courbes la cervelle par les fosses du nez, les entrailles par l'incision pratiquée dans son flanc gauche . . . avant de l'enduire de bitumes et d'essences, lui insèrent, dans les parties sexuelles, pour les purifier, les chastes petals de la divine fleur. (150)

> Des Esseintes puzzled his brains to find the meaning of this emblem. . . . Perhaps he [Moreau, in placing the lotus-blossom

The Unworking of Synaesthesia in Joris-Karl Huysmans's *À Rebours* 79

in Salome's hand] had remembered the sepulchral rites of ancient Egypt, the solemn ceremonies of embalmment, when practitioners and priests lay out the dead woman's body on a slab of jasper, then with curved needles extract her brains through the nostrils, her entrails through an opening made in the left side, and finally . . . before anointing the corpse with oils and spices, insert into her sexual parts, to purify them, the chaste petals of the divine flower. (54)

In the description of *L'Apparition*, the text again moves into the present tense as Salome steps forth; but again, the move of presencing is countered by a certain stabilization: "Dans une geste d'épouvante, Salomé repousse la terrifiante vision qui la cloue, immobile, sur les pointes" (151) ("With a gesture of horror, Salome tries to thrust away the terrifying vision which holds her nailed to the spot, balanced on the tip of her toes") (54). A detailed and vibrant description follows in a play of concealing/revealing. "Dans l'ardeur de la danse," the text continues, "les voiles se sont défaits, les brocarts ont croulé; elle n'est plus vêtue que de matières orfévries et de minéraux lucides" (151) ("In the heat of the dance," the text continues, "her veils have fallen away and her brocade robes slipped to the floor, so that now she is clad only in wrought metals and translucent gems") (54). The figure is brought to full animation as the elements enclosing her are illuminated by the light shining from the head of John the Baptist. It is with the convergence of sight and smell that the moment of seduction—the transgression of the boundary between spectacle and spectator—occurs. Huysmans describes "le Tétrarque, qui . . . halète encore, affolé par cette nudité de femme impregnée de senteurs fauves, roulée dans les baumes, fumée dans les encens et dans les myrrhes" (152) ("the Tetrarch, who, . . . is still panting with emotion, maddened by the sight and smell of the woman's naked body, steeped in musky scents, anointed with aromatic balms, impregnated with incense and myrrh") (55). Like the emptied Egyptian corpse, Salome here smells. Odor and vision collaborate to seduce, or in French the verb is *troubler*: "Tel que le vieux roi, des Esseintes demeurait écrasé, anéanti, pris de vertige, devant cette danseuse, moins majestueuse, moins hautaine, mais plus troublante que la Salomé du tableau à l'huile . . . elle vivait, plus raffinée et plus sauvage, plus execrable et plus exquise; elle réveillait plus énergiquement les sense en léthargie de l'homme, ensorcelait, domptait plus sûrement ses volontés" (152–53) ("Like the old King, Des Esseintes invariably felt overwhelmed, subjugated, stunned when he looked at this dancing-girl, who was less majestic, less haughty, but more seductive than the Salome of the oil-painting . . . here she came to life, more refined yet more savage, more hateful yet more exquisite than before; she roused the sleeping senses of the male more powerfully, subjugated his will more surely with her charms") (55).

The troubling seduction subjugates, stuns. At the same moment, the viewer (des Esseintes) identifies with Herod, thus traversing the frame around the painting and collapsing the difference. The text returns to the past tense as it indicates this identification, thus shielding the reader from the identification it attributes to des Esseintes. Here, the text enframes Salome even as she comes to life within it. At this climactic moment, she again turns into an unmoving image, an actress or entertainer held fast on the scene: "Dans l'insensible et impitoyable statue, dans l'innocente et dangereuse idole, l'érotisme, la terreur de l'être humain s'était fait jour . . . la déesse s'était évanouie; un effroyable chauchemar étranglait maintenant l'histrionne, extasiée par le tournoiement de la danse, la courtisane, pétrifiée, hypnotisée par l'épouvante" (152) ("In the unfeeling and unpitying statue, in the innocent and deadly idol, the lusts and fears of common humanity had been awakened; . . . the goddess vanished; a hideous nightmare now held in its choking grip an entertainer, intoxicated by the whirling movement of the dance, a courtesan, petrified and hypnotized by terror") (55). Moreau's Salome articulates for Huysmans the inseparability of prosopopeia and petrifaction, of bringing to life and killing off—a double movement describing the mirroring relation between text and image.

The allegorical moment aims to transcend time and point beyond itself. Huysmans connects this status of Salome's body to Moreau's relationship to history. Her origin is displaced as she becomes allegorical. Huysmans writes: "Ainsi comprise, elle appartenait aux théogonies de l'extrême Orient; elle ne relevait plus des traditions bibliques . . ." (149) ("Viewed in this light, she belonged to the theogonies of the Far East; she no longer had her origin in biblical tradition . . .") (53). The unworking of Salome's body parallels the dissolution of historical tradition. The depiction of the dance, according to des Esseintes/Huysmans, exceeds the literalness of the letter provided by the skeleton of the story of Salome in the Bible: "Mais ni saint Matthieu, ni saint Marc, ni saint Luc, ni les autres évangélistes ne s'étendait sur les charmes délirants, sur les actives dépravations de la danseuse. Elle demeurait effacée, se perdait, mystérieuse et pâmée, dans le brouillard lointain des siècles" (148) ("But neither St. Matthew, nor St. Mark, nor St. Luke, nor any of the other sacred writers had enlarged on the maddening charm and potent depravity of the dancer. She had always remained a dim and distant figure, lost in a mysterious ecstasy far off in the mists of time") (52). As Meltzer points out, and Huysmans echoes here, the biblical passages either fail to mention the dance or do not describe it in any length or detail; *À Rebours* supplements the biblical accounts. In doing so, according to Huysmans, Moreau loosens the figure from any specific historical setting.

> Le peintre semblait d'ailleurs avoir voulu affirmer sa volonté de rester hors des siècles, de ne point préciser d'origine, de pays, d'époque, en mettant sa Salomé au milieu de cet extraordinaire palais, d'un style confus et grandiose, en la vêtant de somptueuses et chimériques robes, en la mitrant d'un incertain diadème en forme de tour phénicienne tel qu'en porte la Salammbô, en lui plaçant enfin dans la main le sceptre d'Isis, la fleur sacrée de l'Egypte et de l'Inde, le grand lotus. (149)

> Moreover, the painter seemed to have wished to assert his intention of remaining outside the bounds of time, of giving no precise indication of race or country or period, setting as he did his Salome inside this extraordinary palace with its grandiose, heterogeneous architecture, clothing her in sumptuous, fanciful robes, crowning him with a nondescript diadem like Salammbo's, in the shape of a Phoenician tower, and finally putting in her hand the scepter of Isis, the sacred flower of both Egypt and India, the great lotus-blossom. (53)

This metonymic concatenation is often counted by critics as a moment of transcendence of history and of time rather than a collection of varied historical moments, syncretically gathered together and mechanically juxtaposed, but not metaphorically superseded into a unity or whole.

Moreau's art, which Huysmans/des Esseintes describes as "scholarly," is a kind of sociohistorical collation, a syncretic bricolage of diverse historical epochs and cultures. It borrows from the arts of the enameler, the lapidary and the etcher, as well as the art of writing: "Il y avait dans ses œuvres désespérées et érudites un enchantement singulier, une incantation vous remuant jusqu'au fond des entrailles . . . et l'on demeurait ébahi, songeur, déconcerté, par cet art qui franchissait les limites de la peinture, empruntait à l'art d'écrire ses plus subtiles évocations" (154) ("His sad and scholarly work breathed a strange magic . . . so that you were left amazed and pensive, disconcerted by this art which crossed the frontiers of painting to borrow from the writer's art its most subtly evocative suggestions") (56).

The dissolution of the boundaries between genres and media parallels the confusion of art and life through the tense shifts in chapter 5 of *À Rebours*. The senses are concatenated to produce animation and transgression.

A similar animation that transgresses diegetic boundaries occurs in chapter 14, the literary chapter of *À Rebours*. This chapter contains a catalogue of des Esseintes's literary compatriots as well as his definition of the symbol and his characterization of the prose poem as the "osmazome" of literature. In Huysmans's Mallarmé we find again the coordination of figuration, animation, and synaesthesia. Of des Esseintes selection of eleven Mallarmé texts, Huysmans writes: "une entre autres, un fragment de l'*Hérodiade*, le subjuguait de même qu'un sortilège, à certaines heures" (326) ("there was one in particular, a fragment of *Hérodiade*, that seemed to lay a magic spell on him at certain times") (180). The effect of reading as that of a magic spell parallels the magic charm of both the figure of Salome and the art of Moreau. The text continues: "Combien de soirs, sous la lampe éclairant de ses lueurs baissées la silencieuse chambre, ne s'était-il point senti effleuré par cette Hérodiade qui, dans l'œuvre de Gustave Moreau maintenant envie par l'ombre, s'effaçait plus légère, ne laissant plus entrevoir qu'une confuse statue, encore blanche, dans un brasier éteint de pierres!" (326). ("Often of an evening, sitting in the dim light his lamp shed over the silent room, he [des Esseintes] had imagined he felt her brush past him—that same Herodias who in Gustave Moreau's picture had withdrawn into the advancing shadows so that nothing could be seen but the vague shape of a white statue in the midst of a feebly glowing brazier of jewels") (180). Salome, confused here with her mother Herodias, walks through the text at the same narrative level as des Esseintes in his imagination. The figure he draws from Mallarmé and imagines in his house merges vaguely with the figure in the watercolor. The painted image is animated again through the reading of Mallarmé, thus adjoining the painting, Huysmans's novel as the medium of conjunction, and Mallarmé's poem: "Invinciblement, il levait les yeux vers elle, la discernait à ses contours inoubliés et elle revivait, évoquant sur ses lèvres ces bizarres et doux vers que Mallarmé lui prête:

'. . . O miroir!

Eau froide par l'ennui dans ton cadre gelée
Que de fois et pendant des heures, désolée
Des songes et cherchant mes souvenirs qui sont
Comme des feuilles sous ta glace au trou profond,

Je m'apparus en toi comme une ombre lointaine,
Mais, horreur! des soirs, dans ta sévère Fontaine,
J'ai de mon rêve épars connu la nudité!' " (327)

("His eyes were irresistibly drawn towards her, following the familiar outlines of her body until she came to life again before him, bringing to his lips those sweet, strange words that Mallarmé puts into her mouth):

'Oh mirror!

Cold water frozen by boredom in your frame
How many times for hours, desolate
From dreams and searching my memories which are
Like leaves in the deep hole under your ice,
I have appeared in you like a distant shadow,
But horror! Evenings, in your severe fountain,
I have known the nudity of my sparse dream.' "[9]

The synaesthetic convergence of media accompanies the animation of the figure as des Esseintes, enunciating Mallarmé's words, speaks for Salome as she speaks to the reflecting medium of the mirror. Notably, the Mallarmé text des Esseintes privileges is not simply a poem, but a dramatic poem. He lip-synchs a soliloquy from Mallarmé's text, "Hérodiade," a drama in three acts that was never finished or published in its entirety. Des Esseintes quotes from the middle section, called "Scène," that precisely calls into question the ability of the text to make a scene. The play was first published as "Fragment d'une Etude Scénique Ancienne d'un poème de Hérodiade" in 1869. Written in dramatic form, the text features its capacity to conjure forth a figure and make it speak. But if the text's theatricality connects it to prosopopoeia, the preponderance of narrative flattens it out again. The difficulty of acting this scene, or "Scène," overlaps with Hérodiade's difficulty acting; many read this play as Mallarmé's *Hamlet*. We certainly see no dance, though John the Baptist's head is delivered in the "Canticle of Saint John," the final section of the play. Mallarmé himself referred to this text as "Cette pièce de théâtre devenu poème," "This theatrical play become poem." Peter Szondi, in "Sept leçons sur *Hérodiade*," argues that the text is incompatible with the demands of the theater for a number of reasons, one of them being this mixture of narrative (*récit*) and dialogue, and the mixture of present and past tenses that accompanies it.[10]

In the passage re-cited by des Esseintes, Hérodiade turns away from her nurse, the other character in the scene, to address the mirror. The opening apostrophe animates and calls on a dialogic partner only to set it forth as the dull matter of a mirror, "cold water frozen in its frame." The figure of the mirror undercuts the lyric force of the apostrophe, echoing the simultaneous animation and petrifaction of the figure of Salome in Huysmans's text and pointing to the solipsistic quality of self-reflection—the same relation we find in Hérodiade's relation to her own past and her own image in the lines quoted above. She sheds her memories like leaves, performing a figurative striptease as she appears as a distant shadow to herself. The model of specular self-reflection is not completed, that is, the figure does not attain coherence or unity. For Szondi, Hérodiade's fragmentation and the symbolizing reification of her hair belong precisely to those qualities of Mallarmé's text that work against its dramatic presentability and the presencing of the figure of Hérodiade.

While the animation of the figure of Salome/Hérodiade causes Huysman's and Mallarmé's texts to converge, the differences in their writing holds them apart. While the action of the symbol in Mallarmé condenses, Huysmans's expansive cataloging style, like the perfumes Hérodiade dismisses, expands, and envelops. Huysmans writes of Mallarmé,

> Percevant les analogies les plus lointaines, il désignait souvent d'un terme donnant à la fois, par un effet de similitude, la forme, le parfum, la couleur, la qualité, l'éclat, l'objet ou l'être auquel il eût fallu accoler de nombreuses et de différentes épithètes pour en dégager toutes les faces, toutes les nuances, s'il avait été simplement indiqué par son nom technique. Il parvenait ainsi à abolir l'énoncé de la comparaison qui s'établissait, toute seule, dans l'esprit du lecteur, par l'analogie, dès qu'il avait pénétré le symbole, et il se dispensait d'éparpiller l'attention sur chacune des qualités qu'auraient pu presenter, un à un, les adjectifs placés à la queue leu leu, la concentrait sur un seul mot, sur un tout, produisant, comme pour un tableau par example, un aspect unique et complet, un ensemble. (327–328)

> Sensitive to the remotest affinities, he would often use a term that by analogy suggested at once form, scent, colour, quality and brilliance, to indicate a creature or things to which he would have had to attach a host of different epithets in order to bring

out all its various aspects and qualities, if it had merely been referred to by its technical name. By this means he managed to do away with the formal statement of a comparison that the reader's mind made by itself as soon as it had understood the symbol, and he avoided dispersing the reader's attention over all the several qualities that a row of adjectives would have presented one by one, concentrating it instead on a single word, a single entity, producing, as in the case of a picture, a unique and comprehensive impression, an overall view. (181)

The method of Mallarmé's symbolism, assimilated to the creation of a painting (*tableau*), seems to be exactly the contrary of Huysmans's: for his language is paratactic, piling up and accumulating overt comparisons again and again. For example, in this passage, Salome's dismembered body emerges through the animation of stones in a repetitive series of similes.

> les pierres s'animent, dessinnent le corps de la femme en traits incandescents; la piquent au cou, aux jambs, aux bras, de points de feu, vermeils comme des charbons, violets comme des jets de gaz, bleues comme des flames d'alcool, blancs comme des rayons d'astre. (152)

> the stones burn brightly, outlining the woman's figure in flaming colors, indicating neck, legs and arms with points of light, red as burning coals, violet as jets of gas, blue as flaming alcohol, white as moonbeams. (55)

The discussion of the prose poem is pertinent to the functioning of synaesthesia in artistic creation. For des Esseintes/Huysmans, the prose poem is the favored form: "Maniée par un alchimiste de génie, elle devait, suivant lui, renfermer, dans son petit volume . . . la puissance du roman dont elle supprimait les longueurs analytiques et les superfétations descriptives" (330) ("Handled by an alchemist of genius it should . . . contain within its small compass and in concentrated form the substance of a novel, while dispensing with the latter's long-winded analyses and superfluous descriptions") (183). Des Esseintes believes that the novel ought actually to follow the same method as the prose poem and work through the elliptical method of what was previously defined as the symbol: "Alors les mots choisis seraient tellement impermutables qu'ils suppléeraient à tous les autres; l'adjectif . . . ouvrirait de telles perspectives que le lecteur pourrait rêver pendant des semaines entières, sur son sens, tout à la fois précis et multiple, constaterait le présent, reconstruirait le passé, devinerait l'avenir d'âmes des personnages, révélés par les lueurs de cette épithète" (331) ("The words chosen for a work of this sort would be so unalterable that they would take the place of all others; every adjective . . . would open up such wide vistas that the reader could muse on its meaning, at once precise and multiple, for weeks on end, and also reconstruct the past and divine the future of the characters in the light of this one epithet") (183). Thus conceived, "le poème en prose représentait, pour des Esseintes, le suc concret, l'osmazôme de la littérature, l'huile essentielle de l'art. Cette succulence développée et réduite en une goutte, elle existait déjà chez Baudelaire, et aussi dans ces poèmes de Mallarmé qu'il humait avec un si profonde joie" (331) ("the prose poem represented in des Esseintes' eyes the dry juice, the osmazome of literature, the essential oil of art. This succulent extract concentrated in a single drop could already be found in Baudelaire, and also in those poems of Mallarmé's that he savoured with such rare delight") (183–84). The experience of this essence creates a collaboration, a community of readership.

The essence of literature is thus fundamentally related to the senses of taste and smell, to the diffusion of savor and aroma from a concentrated essence. Aroma in particular overcomes or transgresses the boundary between subject and object as its molecules actually exude and enter the body perceiving them. As we saw in the case of Salome, the smells of the body are fundamentally connected to its seductiveness, likewise a crossing over between bodies. The capacity of the aromatic essence to be both specific and to expand into a generality parallels the operation of the symbol. Contrary to traditional aesthetics, des Esseintes includes smell in his doctrine of synaesthesia:

> Il pensait que l'odorat pouvait éprouver des jouissances égales à celles de l'ouïe et de la vue, chaque sens étant susceptible, par suite d'une disposition naturelle et d'une érudite culture, de percevoir des impressions nouvelles, de les décupler, de les coordonner, d'en composer ce tout qui constitue une œuvre; et il n'était pas, en somme, plus anormal qu'un art existât, en dégageant d'odorants fluids, que d'autres, en détachant des ondes sonores, ou en frappant de rayons diversement colorés le rétine d'un œil. (222)

he maintained that the sense of smell could procure pleasures equal to those obtained through sight or hearing, each of the senses being capable, by virtue of a natural aptitude supplemented by an erudite education, of perceiving new impressions, magnifying these tenfold and co-ordinating them to compose the whole that constitutes a work of art. After all, he argued, it was no more abnormal to have an art that consisted of picking out odorous fluids than it was to have other arts based on a selection of sound waves or the impact of variously coloured rays on the retina of the eye. (105)

The affinity between smell and literature is made explicit in chapter 10 of *À Rebours*, in which des Esseintes experiments with perfumes, which are said to possess a language: "Peu à peu, les arcanes de cet art . . . s'étaient ouverts devant des Esseintes, qui déchiffrait maintenant cette langue, variée, aussi insinuante que celle de la littérature, ce style d'une concision inouïe, sous son apparence flottante et vague. Pour cela, il lui avait d'abord fallu travailler la grammaire, comprendre la syntaxe des odeurs" (223–224) ("Little by little the arcana of this art . . . had been revealed to des Esseintes, who could now decipher its complex language that was as subtle as any human tongue, yet wonderfully concise under its apparent vagueness. To do this he first had to master the grammar, to understand the syntax of smells") (106). He has acquired a poetic expertise in smell, a practice called "an interpretation of texts." At the same time, the term *composition* opens up an equivalence between perfumery, music, and poetry. Des Esseintes lets loose various perfumes in the atmosphere of his room, then proceeds "to strike a reverberating chord" (108–9) by adding another scent. Likewise: "Il avait autrefois aimé à se bercer d'accords en parfumerie" (228) ("At one time he had enjoyed soothing his spirit with scented harmonies") (109).

In addition, des Esseintes's aroma-poeisis is equated with the arts of drawing and painting: "Ce décor posé en quelques grandes lignes, fuyant à perte de vue sous ses yeux fermés, il insuffla une légère pluie d'essences" (229) ("Once he had roughed out this background in its main outlines, so that it stretched away into the distance behind his closed eyelids, he sprayed the room with a light rain of essences") (110). Aromatic composition thus connects language, smell, and music. The manipulation of musical and linguistic forms or phrases allows des Esseintes to sketch out a landscape as if sketching or painting: "Actuellement, il voulut vagabonder dans un surprenant et variable paysage, et il débuta par une phrase, sonore, ample, ouvrant tout d'un coup une échapée de campagne immense" (228–229) ("At present his ambition was to wander at will across a landscape full of changes and surprises, and he began with a simple phrase that was ample and sonorous, suddenly opening up an immense vista of countryside") (109). The art of smells explicitly resembles the art of poetry:

> Il usait d'effets analogues à ceux des poètes, employait, en quelque sorte, l'admirable ordannance de certaines pièces de Baudelaire, telles que "l'Irréparable" et "le Balcon" où le dernier des cinq vers qui composent la strophe est l'écho du premier et revient, ainsi qu'un refrain, noyer l'âme dans des infinis de mélancholie et de langueur. Il s'égarait dans les songes qu'évoquaient pour lui ces stances aromatique, ramené soudain à son point de départ, au motif de sa méditation, par le retour du thème initial, reparaissant, à des intervalles ménagés, dans l'odorante orchestration du poème. (228)

> He would use effects similar to those employed by the poets, following as closely as possible the admirable arrangement of certain poems by Baudelaire such as *L'Irréparable* and *Le Balcon*, in which the last of the five lines in each verse echoes the first, returning like a refrain to drown the soul in infinite depths of melancholy and languor. He used to roam haphazardly through the dreams conjured up for him by these aromatic stanzas, until he was suddenly brought back to his starting point, to the motif of his meditation, by the recurrence of the initial theme, reappearing at fixed intervals in the fragrant orchestration of the poem. (109)

The arts of smell, music, and poetry adjoin here in the rhythm of dissemination and return that is both poetic and musical (cf. "Harmonie du Soir": "Valse mélancolique et langoureux vertige!"). The image of unification, however, is but a dream evoked only momentarily.

The structure of dispersion and return belongs alike to smell, music, and poetry. In his aroma-poetic composition in chapter 10, des Esseintes creates a country meadow, which he then fills in with various flowers and scenes. The backdrop acts as a recurrent motif (and Huysmans uses the Wagnerian term), "créant par la fonte et le heurt de tous ces tons, un parfum général, innommé, imprévu, étranger, dans lequel reparaissait, comme un obstiné refrain, la phrase décorative du commencement, l'odeur du grand pré, éventé par les lilas et les tilleuls" (231) ("creating out of the union and collision of all these tones one common perfume [un parfum général], unnamed, unexpected, unusual, in which there reappeared, like a persistent refrain, the decorative phrase he had started with, the smell of the great meadow and the swaying lilacs and linden trees") (111). The word "refrain" applies to both music and poetry, as does the term "ritornel" used here: "Il laisse, par un ventilateur, s'échapper ces ondes odorantes, conservant seulement la campagne qu'il renouvela et dont il força la dose pour l'obliger à revenir ainsi qu'une ritornelle dans ses strophes" (229) (". . . he let these fragrant odours escape through a ventilator, keeping only the country scent, which he renewed, increasing the dose so as to force it to return like a ritornel at the end of each stanza") (110). Like the Wagnerian motif, the return of the original phrase is not magical or mysterious, rather, it is a calculated and mechanically operated technique.

Hallucination alternates with the mechanical know-how that allows des Esseintes to compose and decompose with smells: "Des Esseintes étudiait, analysait l'âme de ces fluids, faisait l'exégèse de ces textes; il se complaisait à jouer pour sa satisfaction personelle, le rôle d'un psychologue, à démontrer et à remonter les rouages d'un œuvre, a dévisser les piècent formant la structure d'une exhalaison composée, et, dans cet exercise, son odorat était parvenu à la sûreté d'une touche presqu'impeccable" (226) ("Des Esseintes studied and analysed the spirit of these compounds and worked on an interpretation of these texts; for his own personal pleasure and satisfaction he took to playing the psychologist, to dismantling the mechanism of a work and reassembling it, to unscrewing the separate pieces forming the structure of a composite odour, and as a result of these operations his sense of smell had acquired an almost infallible flair") (107). Smell and the coarticulation of the arts and senses it enables, do not regress to the state of a mollusk, nor to Freud's four-legged posture. Nor is smell the pre- or extralinguistic sensation it is usually taken for. Rather, smell and the synaesthesia it invokes participate in a technological decomposition that always analyzes what it seems to synthesize.

Chapter 6

Correspond*a*nces

Between Baudelaire and Heidegger

Heidegger's philosophy is a theory of correspondence. This claim is jarring. For was not one of his projects precisely to criticize the correspondence theory of truth?[1] The exchange of letters in my title is meant to invoke the *French* word—the title of Baudelaire's synaesthetic sonnet—and thereby set up a relay between the notion of correspondence (from *adaequatio* to *Entsprechung*) in Heidegger and the mysticism of *correspondances* from Swedenborg to Baudelaire and beyond.[2] But despite the resonance of *Denken und Dichten*, is it not specious to place Heidegger's "philosophy" (by which I mean here what is named in his lecture, "Was ist das—die Philosophie?") in such proximity, in such an affinity, with the metaphysical poetics, or poetical metaphysics, of correspondence? In putting these terms together, I am crossing a line—among other things, the one between German and French. Heidegger crossed this line in 1955, when he delivered his lecture, "Was ist das—die Philosophie?" in Cerisy-La-Salle.[3] In this text, Heidegger performs an interesting self-translation at key moments, retaining the French words in parentheses in the German text, thus not leaving them to the whims of a translator. He explicitly and emphatically translates the term *entsprechen* as *correspondance*, thus inscribing himself in the vocabularies of both the concept of truth as correspondence and the mysticism of poetic *correspondances*. Despite the practices of bracketing or separating prefixes, the resonance of correspondence continues to be heard throughout Heidegger's refashioning of the term as *entsprechen*. I would like here to consider the itinerary of correspondence in Heidegger from the critique of truth as adequation to the infralinguistic relation to Being it comes to be in his later texts.

The Critique of Truth as Correspondence

The theme of Heidegger's critique is consistently the conception of truth as correspondence, as *adaequatio intellectus et rei*, the adequacy of the word to the thing or of a proposition to a state of affairs. Instead, as is well known, Heidegger puts forth the notion of truth as *aletheia*, *Unverborgenheit*, *verbergen/entbergen*, a process of movement of concealing and revealing. Truth as *aletheia* is a "*Grundzug*," a fundamental trait, of being itself, not a characteristic of propositions. There are several things at stake in Heidegger's critique of the concept of truth as adequation that are clearly outlined already in *Sein und Zeit*. First, adequation implies that truth is a proposition, a position that Heidegger denies. Second, it is important that the relation of adequation or assimilation is a relationship of representation. The shift of meaning of "truth" to "correctness" follows the installation of representation that, in turn, sets up a separation and an opposition between subjectivity and objectivity. "*Richtigkeit*" suggests a relation of measurement and calculability that the framework of representation sets up.

Heidegger argues consistently that the locus of truth is not the proposition. Instead, it lies in the relationship or comportment (*Verhalten*) toward being through which the world or *Seiendes* is disclosed. In *Sein und Zeit*, *Being and Time*, Heidegger shows that the relationship between *Da-sein* and *Seiendes*, as truth is prior to and in fact grounds or makes possible the notion of truth as adequation or correspondence. *Erschlossenheit* and *Unverborgenheit* make *homoiosis* possible. In *Sein und Zeit*, Heidegger argues that truth as correspondence is a deficient mode of truth as "discoveredness" (*Entdecktheit*). This is defined specifically as a relation of representation. Given his critique of representation and his obvious rejection of the notion of truth as adequation, it would seem that Heidegger was done with the term *correspondence* altogether. As he writes in *Sein und Zeit*, the traditional concept of truth has been "*ausgeschaltet*" or bracketed out.[4] But it reappears as an "other" correspondence in the term *Entsprechung*, especially as it appears in his 1955 lecture, "Was ist das—die Philosophie?" This lecture was given at Cerisy on the occasion of Heidegger's first visit to France. *Entsprechung* is meant to present an "other" correspondence that is not correspondence. I want to suggest that the introduction of the term

Entsprechung cannot help reintroducing the overtones of correspondence as *homoiosis* that Heidegger wants so much to be done with. Especially in the context of his lecture in France, in which the term is explicitly translated as the French *correspondance*, a large philosophical and poetic tradition is potentially reactivated. That is, *Entsprechung* cannot quite be rid of its sense as "correspondence." The problem becomes salient in working in English, as the terms *adequation*, *correspondence*, and *Entsprechung* become almost impossible to hold apart.

In paragraph 44 of *Sein und Zeit*, Heidegger investigates the inherited meaning of truth as correspondence characteristic of the Western philosophical tradition, begun with Aristotle, that considers philosophy to be a science (*Wissenschaft*, science) of truth (213/256). The canon of understanding truth as correspondence, *adaequatio intellectus et rei*, really gets underway with Thomas of Aquinas, who "gebraucht für adaequatio (Angleichung) auch die Termini correspondentia (Entsprechung) und convenienta (Übereinkunft)" (214) ("uses for '*adaequatio*' [likening] the term *correspondentia* ['correspondence'] and 'conventia' ['coming together']") (257). Rejecting both the notion that the assertion or judgment is the "place" (Ort) of truth, and that truth is based on adequation, Heidegger investigates instead the ontological conditions that make a statement true. Truth as adequation is possible only on the basis of the more "authentic" mode of speech Heidegger describes as the "discovering" quality of the assertion or *Aussage*. He writes,

> Die Aussage ist *wahr*, bedeutet: sie endeckt das Seiende an ihm selbst. Sie sagt aus, sie zeigt auf, sie "lässt sehen" . . . das Seiende in seiner Entdecktheit. *Wahrsein* der Aussage muss verstanden werden als *entdeckt-sein*. Wahrheit hat also gar nicht die Struktur einer Übereinstimmung zwischen Erkennen und Gegenstand im Sinner einer Angleichung eines Seienden (Subjekt) an ein anderes (Objekt). (218–19)

> To say that the assertion "*is true*" signifies that it uncovers the entity as it is in itself. Such an assertion asserts, points out, "lets" the entity "be seen" . . . in its uncoveredness. The *Being-true (truth)* of the assertion must be understood as *Being-uncovered*. Thus truth has by no means the structure of an agreement between knowing and the object in the sense of a likening of one entity (the Subject) to another (the Object). (261)

"Die aletheia," he continues, ". . . bedeutet die Sachen selbst, das, was sich zeigt, das Seiende im Wie siner Endecktheit" (219) (". . . aletheia . . . signifies the 'things themselves'; it signifies what shows itself—*entities in the 'how' of their uncoveredness*") (262).

Heidegger echoes here Husserl's call to return to "the things themselves" in pointing to a conception of truth that joins language (logos, *Sprache* as *Aussage*) and *Sache* immediately.[5] Because of the iterability of language, that is, its capacity to be repeated without repeating the gesture it performs, a statement can decay into a mere "Vorhandendes," an entity that is. In this way, truth as correspondence develops out of the genuine relationship of logos and *Sache* into a mere entity itself, a relation between two entities.

> Entdecktheit von . . . wird zur vorhandenen Gemässheit eines Vorhandenen, der ausgesprochenen Aussage, zu Vorhandenem, dem besprochenen Seienden. Und wird die Gemässheit nur mehr noch als Beziehung zwischen Vorhandenen gesehen . . . dann zeigt sich der Bezug als vorhandenes Übereintstimmung zweier Vorhandener. (224)

> The uncoveredness of something becomes the present-at-hand conformity of one thing which is present-at-hand—the entity under discussion. And if this conformity is seen only as a relationship between things which are present-at-hand . . . then the relation shows itself as an agreement of two things which are present-at-hand, an agreement which is present-at-hand itself. (267)

In "Vom Wesen der Wahrheit," "On the Essence of Truth," Heidegger specifies that this is a relationship of representation: "Die vorstellende Aussage sagt ihr Gesagtes so vom vorgestellten Ding, w i e es als dieses ist. Das 'so—wie' betrifft das Vor-stellen und sein Vor-gestelltes. Vor-stellen bedeutet hier . . . das Entgegenstehenlassen des Dinges als Gegenstand"[6] ("What is stated by the presentative statement is said of the presented thing in just such manner *as* that thing, as presented, is. The 'such-as' has to do with the presenting and its presented . . . to present here means to let the thing stand opposed as object") (*Basic Writings*, 121). Through the common medium of representation, subject and object are assimilated to each other in the model of truth as correspondence. This characterizes the language of "*das man*," who no longer experiences the genuine relation between language and thing, but instead compares only represented entities. Truth as correspondence compares entities side by side, that is, horizontally, and not with a view toward being. Otherwise, the impossible demand is made to connect unlike entities. In "Vom Wesen der Wahrheit," Heidegger considers the example of the statement "Dieses Geldstück ist rund" ("The coin is round") (120). The statement would be true if it agrees with or corresponds to the piece of money lying on the table. But Heidegger asks,

> Worin sollen aber das Ding and die Aussage übereinkommen, wo doch die Bezongenen offensichtlich ih ihrem Aussehen verschieden sind? Das Geldstück ist aus Metall. Die Aussage ist überhaupt nicht stofflich. . . . Und dieses Stimmen soll nach dem geläufigen Begriff der Wahrheit eine Angleichung sein. Wie kann das völlig Ungleiche, die Aussage, an das Geldstück sich angleichen? (180–81)

> But wherein are the thing and the statement supposed to be in accordance, considering that the relata are manifestly different in their outward appearance? The coin is made of metal. The statement is not material at all. . . . And according to the usual concept of truth this accord is supposed to be a correspondence. How can what is completely dissimilar, the statement, correspond to the coin? (*Basic Writings*, 120)

This connection, which crosses over from language to thing, must be something other than assimilation, adequation, or correspondence, Heidegger claims.

In "Was ist das—die Philosophie?" Heidegger points to the Greek language as the medium in which thing and language meet. Greek is privileged as a language that immediately is what it signifies.

> Wenn wir jetzt . . . auf Worte der griechischen Sprache hören, dann begeben wir uns in einen ausgezeichneten Bereich. Langsam dämmert nämlich für unsere Besinnung, daß die griechesche Sprache keine bloße Sprache ist wie die uns bekannten europäischen Sprachen. Die griechische Sprache, und sie allein, ist logos . . . Für den Beginn genüge der Hinweis, dass in der griechischen Sprache das in ihr Gesagte auf eine ausgezeichnete Weise zugleich das ist, was das Gesagte nennt . . . Wir sind durch

das griechisch gehörte Wort unmittelbar bei der vorliegenden Sache selbst, nicht zunächst bei einer bloßen Wortbedeutung.[7]

If we listen now . . . to the words of the Greek language, then we move into a distinct and distinguished domain. Slowly it will dawn upon our thinking that the Greek language is no mere language like the European languages known to us. The Greek language, and it alone, is *logos* . . . in the Greek language what is said in it *is* at the same time in an excellent way what it is called . . . Through the audible Greek word we are directly in the presence of the thing itself, not first in the presence of a mere word sign.

In *Sein und Zeit*, Heidegger also points to the unity of logos and truth in Heraklitis.

Also gehört zum λογος die Unverborgenheit, die a-letheia. Die Übersetzung durch das Wort "Wahrheit" und erst recht die theoretischen Begriffsbestimmungen dieses Ausdruckes verdecken den Sinn dessen, was die Griechen als vorphilosophisches Verständnis dem terminologischen Gebrauch von aletheia 'selbstverständlich' zugrunde legen. (219)

Thus to the λογοσ belongs unhiddenness—α-ληθεια. To translate this word as 'truth,' and, above all, to define this expression conceptually in theoretical ways, is to cover up the meaning of what the Greeks made 'self-evidently' basic for the terminological use of αληθεια as a pre-philosophical way of understanding it. (262)

Heidegger listens to this logos, despite, as he claims, guarding against possible "Wortmystik" in the Greek. What is this kind of *Wortmystik* but the notion of an immediate concurrence of word and thing, a pretranslation originality of saying and being?—of a mystical "correspondence"?

In the correspondence of "Was ist das—die Philosophie?," even in this joining there is a difference between the name and the thing. They are not identical, but relate to each other in the mode of resounding harmony or accord. The love of wisdom—Greek "philosophy"—is this originary harmonizing: "'omologein, so sprechen, wie der logos spricht, d.h. dem logos entsprechen. Dieses Entsprechen steht im Einklang mit dem sofon" (46) ("Philein, to love, signifies here, in the Heraclitean sense, homologein, to speak in the way in which the logos speaks, in correspondence with the Logos. This correspondence is in accord with the sophon") (47). One might think that the fall of correspondence takes place in the translation from the privileged Greek into the Latin of tradition.[8] Despite the positive valuing of *homologein* in "Was ist," the difference though is not between Greek and Latin, but rather inheres already in Greek as Heidegger traces it in "Platons Lehre von der Wahrheit."[9] In this essay, Heidegger suggests that the understanding of truth as *aletheia*, *Unverborgenheit*, predates its redefinition as *orthotes*, or *Richtigkeit*, in Plato. *Unverborgenheit*, the capacity of things to shine forth and give themselves as they are, is determined in relation to *Verborgenheit* or a *Sichverbergen*, from which the truth is wrested. *Unverborgenheit* is a "Zug des Seienden" itself, not a quality of knowledge, statement or mind. Plato, argues Heidegger, makes the idea, the principle of something showing itself for what it is (the idea of the "good"), into the origin of both beauty and truth. The idea is thus an object of knowledge, not a trait of being itself. With this migration of the truth from the side of things to knowing, truth is reorganized as the matching of the two: truth as *homoiosis*, adequation or assimilation between mind and thing or statement and fact.

> In diesem Wandel des Wesens der Wahrheit vollzieht sich zugleich ein Wechsel des Ortes der Wahrheit. Als Unverborgenheit ist sie noch ein Grundzug des Seienden selbst. Als Richtigkeit des 'Blickens' aber wird sie zur Auszeichnung des menschlichen Verhaltens zum Seienden.[10]

> With this transformation of the essence of truth there takes place at the same time a change of the locus of truth. As unhiddenness, truth is still a fundamental trait of beings themselves. But as the correctness [137] of the 'gaze,' it becomes a characteristic of human comportment toward beings.[11]

In Plato, then, *aletheia* differs from itself, being both the unexamined (*selbstverständliche*) *Unverborgenheit* that is surpassed and the *orthotes* that results from the "Wandel des Wesens der Wahrheit" of his epoch. This shift takes place as the focus moves, in the allegory of the cave, from the things on the earth to the sun as the "image" of the idea of the good. As soon as the binary between mind and thing is installed, *Unverborgenheit* gives way to *Richtigkeit*, *aletheia* to *veritas*. Heidegger pins his thinking to historical moments marked out as stages on the way of translation: of crossing over from the Being of entities to the relation between subject and object.[12]

Still, somehow *orthotes* continues to be read as truth, *aletheia*, as correspondence, as a relation between two represented entities (subject and object), rather than as the condition of shining forth wrested out of the concealment of *Sichverbergen*. The model of *Unverborgenheit*, though, might be seen as a kind of phenomenological realism: things appear or shine forth as what they really are, or essence allows things to shine forth. If *Verborgenheit* is its condition of possibility, it is not as something to which the revealed should measure up or match.

Entsprechung

In his later texts, Heidegger turns to the topic of correspondence (*Entsprechung*) as the very definition of philosophy. Here, however, the term does not translate to *adaequatio*, *convenienta*, or any of its Latinate relatives. Instead, Heidegger translates the term backward into the Greek as *homologein*. What makes *homologein* different from *adequatio*, or correspondence from correspondence? The thin line between Greek and Latin terms is transgressed in the doubling of the term *correspondence*. This is notable in Heidegger's essay, "Was ist das—die Philosophie?" in the way that French terms are retained and asserted, in particular the term "*correspondance*." The binary of translation is disabled and the distinction between originary and derivative collapses. The border is crossed: Heidegger comes to France.

As the title makes clear, "Was ist das—die Philosophie?" gets underway as a question about the nature of philosophy. Philosophy is not understood as a science of truth; in fact, the question of truth does not arise in the lecture. Heidegger presents philosophy as a conversation, "ein Gespräch."[13] The German term maintains the root for *language*, of course, and takes on the collective form that Heidegger choses elsewhere for "Gestell," for example, which he compares with "Gebirg" and similar terms. In asking the title's question, the text performs the philosophical movement that it is hoping to define. A certain reflexivity is set up that will not be resolved in terms of adequation or agreement between subject and predicate. Instead, the answer to the question opens up as a kind of cospeaking in dialogue.

Wann ist die Antwort auf die Frage: was ist das—die Philosophie? eine philosophierende? Wann philosophieren wir? Offenbar erst dann, wenn wir mit den Philosophen ins Gespräch kommen. Dazu gehört, daß wir mit ihnen dasjenige durchsprechen, wovon sie sprechen. Dieses miteinander-Durchsprechen dessen, was immer wieder als das Selbe die Philosophen eigens angeht, ist das Sprechen, das legein im Sinne des dialegesthai, das Sprechen als Dialog. (66)

When is the answer to the question, "What is philosophy?" a philosophizing one? When do we philosophize? Obviously only when we enter into a discussion with philosophers. This implies that we talk through with them that about which they speak. This mutual talking through off what always anew peculiarly concerns philosophers as being the Same, that is talking, *legein*, in the sense of *dialegesthai* [*sic*.] [conversing], is talking as dialogue. (67)

The discussion is truly one when it takes up "das Selbe," what remains the same, in the concern of philosophy throughout the ages. Despite all the historical differences that can be established through the description of philosophical doctrines, something remains the same.

Wir dürfen aber auch nicht darüber hinweggehen, daß die Philosophie von Aristoteles bis Nietzsche gerade auf dem Grunde dieser Wandlungen und durch sie hindruch dieselbe bleibt. Denn die Verwandlungen sind die Bürgschaft für die Verwandtschaft im Selben. (60)

At the same time we ought not, however, overlook the fact that philosophy from Aristotle to Nietzsche, precisely because of these changes throughout their course, has remained the same. For the transformations are the warranty for the kinship in the same. (61)

Philosophy as conversation allows the same to resound in this affinity. The articulation of this affinity in question and answer is the discussion that is philosophy, is the correspondence to the same, namely, the Being of beings (Sein des Seienden): "Wir finden die Antwort auf die Frage, was die Philosophie sei, nicht durch historische Aussagen über die Definitionen der

Philosophie, sondern durch das Gespräch mit dem, was sich uns als Sein des Seienden überliefert hat" (70) ("We find the answer to the question, 'What is philosophy?' not through historical assertions about the definitions of philosophy but through conversing with that which has been. Handed down to us as the Being of being") (71).

Philosophy is a conversation with Being itself. Through tradition, the Being of being appeals to us (*uns zuspricht*); "indem wir auf diesen Zuspruch hören, gelangen wir in die Entsprechung" (72) ("By listening to this interpellation we attain the correspondence") (73).

There is a peculiar doubling of correspondence here, for it characterizes both the attentiveness to the appeal (*Zuspruch*) and the relationship in which it results. That is, we are always already in correspondence to the call of being, though often we do not attend to it (cf. 74). Philosophy consists in the attentive development of the correspondence to Being in which we already stand: "Das Entsprechen zum Sein des Seienden ist die Philosophie; sie ist es aber erst dann und nur dann, wenn das Entsprechen sich eigens vollzieht, dadurch sich entfaltet und diese Entfaltung ausbaut" (74) ("Philosophy is the correspondence to the Being of being, but until, and only when, the correspondence is actually fulfilled and thereby unfolds itself and expands this unfoldment") (75).

The unfolding development of correspondence is the opening of question and answer, "genuinely understood." This is constituted not by statements about something, but rather by a movement of thinking itself: "Wir selber müssen dem, wohin die Philosophie unterwegs ist, durch unser Denken entgegenkommen. Unser Sprechen muß dem, wovon die Philosophen angesprochen sind, ent-sprechen. Wenn uns dieses Ent-sprechen glückt, dann ant-worten wir im echten Sinne auf die Frage, Was ist das—die Philosophie? Das deutsche Wort 'antworten' bedeutet eigentlich soviel wie ent-sprechen. . . . Die Antwort ist keine erwidernde Aussage (n'est pas une réponse), die Antwort ist vielmehr die Ent-sprechung (la correspondance), die dem Sein des Seienden entspricht" (68) (Heidegger supplies the French terms in parentheses here) ("We must then ourselves, through our thinking, go to meet philosophy on the path it is traveling. Our speaking must co-respond to that which addresses the philosophers. If this co-responding is successful for us, then, in the true sense of the word, we respond to the question, 'What is philosophy?' The German word *antworten* [answer to, *sic*] actually means the same as ent-sprechen [to respond, *sic*]. . . . The answer is not a reply [*n'est pas une réponse*], the answer is rather the co-respondence [*la correspondance*] which responds to the Being of being" [Heidegger supplies the French terms in parentheses]) (69).

Question and answer are gestures or acts, not statements about facts or states of affairs. This gesture of heeding the call is a kind of "event." The unity of philosophy comes across as a reverberation of events like this, in the "Verwandtschaft" of the same. The horizontal relationship between propositions in different historical discourses (philosophy) is replaced by this repetition of a vertical relationship to the true Conversation in which the Being of beings is accessed (in whatever attunement, *Stimmung*). Correspondence names this relationship.[14] Correspondence resounds, however, only when the conversation (*das Gespräch*) is genuine. The question of conversation can always be "eine Scheinfrage zum Zweck einer Konversation" (42) ("a hypothetical question for the purpose of making conversation") (43). Let's say *discussion* might be a better term: to dash or shake to pieces.[15] The concentration on the philosophical discussion bears with it its Romanic counterpart, *Ent-sprechung*, its correspondence, which does not quite correspond.[16] In the same way, as presented above, truth as correspondence is an inauthentic derivative of *aletheia*.

The dissonance or noncorrespondence, the difference, between the German and the French terms is brought to our attention especially when Heidegger inserts French words into his German text. This first occurs when Heidegger describes the kind of relationship we would have to a genuine conversation rather than the empty "Scheinfrage" of Konversation: "Der Weg unserer Gespräche muß also von einer Art und Richtung sein, daß das, wovon die Philosophie handelt, uns selbst angeht, uns berührt (nous touche), und zwar in unserem Wesen" (22) ("The path of our discussion must, therefore, be of such a kind and direction that that of which philosophy treats concerns us personally, affects us and, indeed, touches us (*nous touche*) in our very nature" (23, translation emended). The indication of this point of convergence that is philosophy cannot be translated, apparently, but calls for a double iteration in the French and the German. The text itself is touched by the materiality and heterogeneity of languages. The double language introduces here a difference in the same, or holds open the difference that allows agreement, *homologein*, correspondence, to occur. The difference is the difference of touching, passion, pathos, affection. Insofar as we are touched, philosophy is opened up to this realm. "Aber wird die Philosophie dadurch nicht zu einer Sache der Affektion, der Affekte und der Gefühle?" (22) ("But does not philosophy thereby become a matter of affection, emotions, and sentiments?") (23). In the course of the essay, this pathos will be redefined as *thauma*, the originary pathos of philosophy. In the meantime, an other affect is opened up that is not simply the realm of the irrational (or extrarational) in opposition to ratio as the presumed region of philosophy.

> Wenn wir andererseits auf die Möglichkeit hinweisen, daß das, worauf die Philosophie sich bezieht, uns Menschen in unserem Wesen angeht und uns be-rührt, dann könnte es sein, daß diese Affektion durchaus nichts mit dem zu tun hat, was man gewöhnlich Affekte und Gefühle, kurz das Irrationale nennt. (24–26)

> If, on the other hand, we point out the possibility that that upon which philosophy bears concerns us humans in our essential nature and touches us, then it might be that this affection has nothing whatsoever to do with that which is usually called affects and feeling, in short, the irrational. (Translation emended, 25–27)

Heidegger's use of French terms in the essay "Was ist das—die Philosophie?" thus holds open the difference that makes *correspondance* possible. The materiality of language and the limit of translation, the persistence of untranslatability, prevent the term *correspondance* from turning into a term of identity. Instead, it names a relation that sublimates the ear into its sensed sense of attunement.

> Das Ent-sprechen hört auf die Stimme des Zuspruchs. Was sich als Stimme des Seins uns zuspricht, be-stimmt unser Entsprechen. 'Entsprechen' heist dann: be-stimmt sein, être disposé, nämlich vom Sein des Seienden her. Dis-posé bedeuted hier wörtlich: auseinander-gesetzt, gelichtet und dadurch in die Bezüge zu dem versetzt, was ist. (76)

> The correspondence listens to the voice of the appeal. What appeals to us as the voice of Being evokes our correspondence. "Correspondence" then means: being determined, *être disposé* by that which comes from the Being of being. *Dis-posé* here means literally set-apart, cleared, and thereby placed in relationship with what is. (77)

The punctuation of German by French enacts the being opened apart of attunement itself.

Correspondence brings about the division that one might think it was supposed to overcome. But to do this, it remains dependent on the contingencies of different languages, of French and German and their specific and singular material features that cling to the uniqueness of enunciation. As this dependency surfaces, Heidegger must shore up the defense of the necessary against the threat of the realm of affections and feelings (not feeling).

> Das Entsprechen ist notwending und immer, nicht nur zufällig und bisweilen, ein gestimmtes. . . . Als ge-stimmtes und be-stimmtes ist das Entsprechen wesenhaft in einer Stimmung. Dadurch ist unser Verhalten jeweils so oder so gefügt. Die so verstandene Stimmung ist keine Musik von zufällig auftauchenden Gefühlen, die das Entsprechen nur begleiten. Wenn wir die Philosophie als das gestimmte Entsprechen kennzeichnen, dann wollen wir keineswegs das Denken dem zufälligen Wechsel und den Schwankungen von Gefühlszuständen ausliefern. (76–78)

> Correspondence is necessary and is always attuned, and not just accidentally and occasionally. . . . As something tuned and attuned, correspondence really exists in a tuning. Through it our attitude is adjusted sometimes in this, sometimes in that way. The tuning understood in this sense is not music of accidentally emerging feelings which only accompany the correspondence. If we characterize philosophy as tuned correspondence, then we by no means want to surrender thinking to the accidental changes and vacillations of sentiments. (77–79)

Correspondence should not be engendered by the resonating parts, should not be turned out (ausgeliefert) and delivered over to the vicissitudes of sensations or feelings, but should only come about by heeding the call of being. But how to prevent this other kind of resonance, the resounding of feelings, of specific sayings of separate languages? In a strange moment of self-assertion, Heidegger makes a claim for the unity of correspondence in the draw and claim of Being by allowing the linguistic subject to show and reiterating the sameness/difference of Entsprechen and *correspondance*: "Vielmehr handelt es sich einzig darum, darauf hinzuweisen, daß jede

Präzision des Sagens in einer Disposition des Entsprechens gründet, des Entsprechens sage ich, der correspondance, im Achten auf den Zuspruch" (78) ("It is rather solely a question of pointing out that every precision of language is grounded in a disposition of correspondence, of *correpondance*, I say, in heeding the appeal") (79, translation emended).

This is a very odd sentence. Strangely, Heidegger maintains the latinate "Disposition" to rename Stimmung, mood or attunement, thus disarticulating it or giving it a kind of double character. For once, the Latin based word seems to capture something that escapes the German word. Perhaps we find here the reversal of what Heidegger says in his *Spiegel* interview of the 1960s: "I am thinking of the special inner kinship between the German language and the language of the Greeks and their thought. This is something that the French confirm for me again and again today. When they begin to think, they speak German. They assure [me] that they do not succeed with their own language."[17] But here: when Heidegger ceases to think—that is, when the specific material contingencies of difference, of the neighboring languages of French and German dominate and occlude the philosophical orientation toward the call or address of Being—he begins to speak French. The assertion of the "ich" and the repetition and duplication of *Entsprechen*/*correspondance* suggest a sense of helplessness, of the text losing control of its language(s), of the borders dissolving. If *Entsprechen* names the correspondence to the Being of beings (as philosophy), correspondence names the relation between *Entsprechen* and *correspondance*—a relation of answering resonance that remains different from itself.

If we look at it this way, correspondence would be a relationship not of mirroring identity, but of differing Sameness, like "the Same" that all philosophers discuss (as quoted above). The "Same"—*das Selbe*—would be the sameness of reverberation, resonance or rhythm: that is, a similarity or unity that is produced temporarily through the interaction of many, whether tones, beats, echoes, and so forth. It requires a plurality and a motion, like a vibrating string, or like the "vaste et profonde unité" performed by the varying echoes in Baudelaire's *Correspondances*. Or it might be like the *laughter* that occurs with understanding or concurrence: a heaving and pealing of the body that comes together in the broken sounds it emits.

In his Lectures on Heraclitus's doctrine of Logos, Heidegger glosses the term "homologein" to mean *not* to say what the other says, but rather, to speak as the other speaks. This bespeaks a basic kind of commingling that has a shared concern: what Heidegger here calls "Einverständnis," or agreement.

Homologia ist das zugestehende, eingestehende Einverständnis. Das Einverständnis besteht also nicht darin, daß im einen and im anderen die gleiche Meinung lebt und vorkommt, sondern daß der eine Mensch und der andere als die Verschiedenen, die sie sind, übereinkommen darin, daß sie sich das Selbe eingestehen als Solches, was sie angeht.[18]

Homologein is the conceding, acknowledging concordance. Concordance, therefore, does not consist in the same opinion existing in both the one and the other, but rather in the fact that one human and the other, as distinct individuals, are in agreement with each other in acknowledging that the same thing addresses them both. (191)

This agreement depends on difference.

The difference between *Entsprechen* and *correspondance* is irreducible, and because of that the two words can resonate or "correspond." In this sense, like the senses in Baudelaire's poem, French, German, and English "respond" to each other: thus stand in a relation of synaesthesia. They are not sublated as instances of an identical meaning, but rather persist as resonating or echoing tones that touch either other. The persistence of the senses holds apart the finality of synaesthesia, just as the resonating differences of languages holds open the single-minded listening to the call of Being that marks out philosophy.

In later essays focused on language in which Heidegger elucidates the term *Entsprechen*, the relationship of harmonious *Einklang* attributed to philia replaces and displaces the subject-object relationship implied in the structure of philosophy as a discourse of truth/knowledge. Language, *die Sprache*, is seen as a nonhuman element that addresses itself to humans (*der Mensch und die Sterblichen*). Rather than the accord between language and thing at which adequation aims, the relation of *Ent-sprechung* intercalates "mortals" and something "other" (*die Sprache*) in the relationship of *Fügung*. "Die Sprache spricht," writes Heidegger in the essay "Die Sprache," "Der Mensch spricht, insofern er der Sprache entspricht."[19] "Man speaks in that he responds [entspricht] to language."[20] This *Entsprechung* is a responding that is secondary, that re-acts to the movement of language and thus has its origin outside itself. Between *sprechen der Sprache* and *Entsprechen des Menschen* there is a kind of rhythmic interruption, a discontinuity in a reflexive relation punctuated by otherness. This is in part what Werner Hamacher indicates by the term *für* in his essay "Für—die Philologie." *Für* points to the relation to an other always characteristic of philology as a kind of companion to language. Hamacher equates *für* with *philia* (70), thus with the kind of speaking in relation to the speaking of logos—*homologein*—that sets up co-respondance.[21] It points to the un-self-contained character of even the self-relation of "die Sprache spricht," which Hamacher redacts (*rezipiert*) as: "Für—die Sprache—spricht" (67) ("*For*—language—speaks") (148). Through *entsprechen*, language opens up alterity and the very possibility of itself as relation, a possibility that can never be marked by a proper name or represented in any term. Hamacher writes that without the syncopation opened up by the "Für" of language as *philia*, language (könnte nicht) "das Feld des Ansprechbaren erschliessen, noch könnte sie der Andersheit, der unpromgrammierbaren künkftigkeit und der möglichen Unansprechbarkeit des von ihr Angesprochenen entsprechen"[22] (Language could not "open up the field of the addressable, nor could it correspond to the otherness, the unprogrammable futurity, and the possible unaddressability of what it addresses") (150). Language misspeaks or unspeaks (*entspricht*) the very thing it co-responds to (*entspricht*); it opens up the otherness to which it stands in an inarticulate relation: "Nur in diesem vierfachen Sinn ist Für das Wort für eine Sprache, die nicht nur Vorhandenes registriert und kommuniziert, sondern alteritäts- und geschichsstoffen noch demjenigen—auch in ihr selbst—zugewandt bleibt, das in keinem Wort keiner Sprache gefasst werden kann" (70) ("Only in this fourfold sense is 'for' the word for a language that does not only register and communicate what is at hand but rather, open to alterity and history, still remains turned toward a word—even one within language—that can be grasped in no word of no language") (150).

The word *für/ for* is able to function this way in part because it "speaks as a homophonic variant" of the French word *fur*, as in *au fur et à mesure*, which Hamacher glosses as "nicht nur 'je nachdem' und 'in dem Masse wie,' sie besagt auch 'entsprechend'—und dieses 'entsprechen' kann seinerseits . . . in ein 'ent-sprechend' . . . verwandelt werden" (68) ("not only . . . 'as the case may be' and 'to the extent.' It also means 'correspondingly' [*entsprechend*]—and this 'correspondingly' can in turn be transformed . . . into an 'un-responding' [*ent-sprechend*] and further . . . into an 'un-wording' " (148).

That is, the word for correspond does not correspond to the word *für* and this noncorrespondence is a kind of de-formation or un-speaking (*Entsprechung* or *Ent-wortung*). Perhaps the same relationship obtains between correspondence (*Entsprechung*) and *correspondance*.

Correspondances

Perhaps I have set up here a rather difficult juggling game among French, German, and English, among philosophical and poetic connotations, that confuses as much as it may elucidate. Yet there is always some vestige of similarity among these terms and tones that allows them to be compared, some sense in which they *correspond*. For Baudelaire, one has no need of doctrine to recognize this affinity. In an 1856 letter to Toussenel he writes: "*L'homme raisonable* n'a pas attendu que Fourier vînt sur la terre pour comprendre que la Nature est un *verbe,* une allégorie, un moule, un *repoussé* si vous voulez. Nous savons cela, et ce n'est pas par Fourier que nous le savons:—nous le savons par nous-mêmes et par les poètes"[23] ("*Rational man* did not wait for Fourier to come to earth to understand that Nature is a *word*, an allegory, a mold, an *embossment,* if you like. We know this, and it is not by way of Fourier that we know it:—we know it by ourselves and by the poets" (my translation). That is, the very relation of intertextual dependence or doctrinal influence depends on the recognition of similarity, the resonance of correspondence, that is in question. Correspondence disseminates itself and in the process becomes unrecognizable, unassimilable to unity or origin. In "Anthropomorphism and Trope," Paul de Man reads "Correspondances" against the grain, finding difference and discord where the traditional doctrine of correspondence would preach harmony or unity. In the important reading of the dissemination of the final simile in the poem, in which the *comme* of simile shifts to the *comme* of never-ending enumeration, de Man inserts the following sentence in French: "Ce comme n'est pas un comme comme les autres," betraying the reliance on similarity and correspondence of even the establishment of difference (*Rhetoric of Romanticism*, 249).

A Note on Rhythm

At the end of chapter 1, I wrote, "Synaesthesia is the extended medium of rhythm." As I have argued throughout this book, this implies that synaesthesia is the rhythmic coarticulation of the senses and the arts that are not organized hierarchically or unified in a totalizing whole. "Synaesethesia," for me, does not name a thing or a condition as a "genuine" originary unity, but rather an area in which a multiplicity can articulate itself. For this reason, I have not departed from a unified definition of synaesthesia that is then exemplified in each chapter. Instead, I have allowed synaesthesia to concatenate the senses and the arts in a variety of contexts with more of an ear for how it functions, rather than what it "is." This shift in emphasis has as much to do with the notion of rhythm as with that of synaesthesia.

Rhythm, like repetition, has no beginning, but only emerges as such in its recapitulation or reiteration, the point at which it becomes recognizable as a pattern. Extending in time and space, it echoes finitude and points to the irrecoverability of origin. Rhythm has to do with the arts in being a function of the senses and the body, being a vibration of movement prior to the specular recognition of the subject by itself. This is what makes rhythm an apt figure for analyzing the social realm.[1] Emile Benveniste defines rhythm as a form or image (Gk. σχημα) that is originally in motion: rhythm "designates the form in the instant that it is assumed by what is moving, mobile and fluid, the form of that which does not have organic consistency; it fits the pattern of a fluid element, of a letter arbitrarily shaped, of a robe which one arranges at one's will, of a particular state of character or mood. It is the form as improvised, momentary, changeable" (285–86).

A mark of finitude, rhythm spaces out the subject and allows it to come to itself, as a return. In his monumental study, *Critique du rythme*, Henri Meschonnic writes that rhythm is such a return: "le retour de la temporalité sur elle-même, du sens sur lui-même, du je sur lui-même" (87) ("The return of temporality upon itself, of sense upon itself, of the I upon itself") (my translation). But crucial is precisely the *absence* of rhythm, the missing original of repetition that allows a self or an image to come into view. Meschonnic quotes Paul Valéry as follows: "'C'est un mode de mouvement . . . le mouvement plus ou moins caché par lequel ce qui n'est pas encore est déjà, ou est entièrement dans ce qui est—s'appelle rythme'" (174) ("It is a mode of movement . . . the movement more or less hidden by which that which is not yet, is already, or is entirely in what is—is called rhythm") (my translation). Rhythm thus disturbs presence, or depresences it. In his magisterial essay, "The Echo of the Subject," Philippe Lacoue-Labarthe writes: "Rhythm, then, is heard. It is not seen . . . rhythm, of a specifically musical (acoustic) essence here, is prior to the figure or the visible schema whose appearance, as such—its very possibility of being perceived—it conditions. This is why its lack throws off (scopic) perception, and *estranges*, defamiliarizes, disturbs the familiar, the visible, the phenomenal, properly speaking" (194). This lack is the lack of origin that characterizes rhythm. Lacoue-Labarthe continues, "The absence of rhythm . . . is equivalent to the infinitely paradoxical appearance of *the mimetic itself*. . . . The absence of that on the basis of which there is imitation, the absence of the imitated or the repeated . . . reveals what is by definition unrevealable—imitation or repetition. . . . *Nothing* occurs" (195).

The occurrence of this "Nothing" in the rhythm of synaesthesia defamiliarizes origin, thus decomposes the unity that used to be signified by synaesthesia. It is a desubtantialization of presence. Like Lacoue-Labarthe, Nancy describes this in the very structure of the self: "Listening is passing over to the register of presence to self, it being understood that 'self' is precisely nothing available (substantial or subsistent) to which one can be 'present,' but precisely the resonance of a return [*renvoi*]" (*Listening*, 12). Music, or the acoustic, is perhaps a privileged figure within a model of what is basically synaesthesia, or the ability of the arts to interact with one another. Nancy writes: "The musical interprets the mutual resonances of artistic and/or perceptible registers [Baudelaire's 'correspondences']. Or else, that if each register is able to interpret these resonances and the generality of resonance, it interprets itself musically every time; thus we can speak of mutual colorations of the friction of the arts or of the senses as modalities of a co-respondence whose paradigm remains sonorous" (*Listening*, 32; Nancy's brackets). Rhythm thus characterizes the realization of what I have called the other synaesthesia.

Notes

Introduction

1. Jacques Derrida has critiqued this metaphysical model of metaphor thoroughly in his magisterial essay, "White Mythology: Metaphor in the Text of Philosophy" in *Margins of Philosophy*. Paul Gordon discusses the problem of metaphor and synaesthesia at length in *Synaesthetics: Art as Synaesthesia*, the most interesting work on synaesthesia to appear in recent years. Gordon argues that all art is synaesthetic. *Synaesthetics* presents an illuminating discussion of Derrida and Heidegger on the metaphysics of metaphor. Paul de Man likewise critiques the hierarchy of literal and figurative suggested by the scientific literature on synaesthesia. See, for example "Semiology and Rhetoric" in *Allegories of Reading*. For very helpful summaries of both the neuroscientific literature on synaesthesia and discussions of the relationship between synaesthesia and metaphor, see Dani Cavallaro, *Synesthesia and the Arts*.

2. I am grateful to Jared Lindahl and Polina Dimova, both of whom pointed me toward this article. Lindahl generously shared references to the neuroscientific literature informing this book, including Simon Baron-Cohen and John E. Harrison, *Synaesthesia: Classic and Contemporary Readings*; Robertson and Sagiv, *Synesthesia: Perspectives from Neuroscience*; and Ward and Mattingly, "Synaesthesia: An Overview of Contemporary Findings and Controversies." These all share an interest in demonstrating that synaesthesia is in fact a neurological condition with physiological underpinnings, and not just the whims of individuals.

Chapter 1

1. For a contextualization of Nancy's work within contemporary theory of community, see Ignaas Devisch. *La Communauté désouevrée* began as an essay published in a special issue of the journal *Aléa* devoted to the topic "Communauté, nombre," in 1983. It was republished along with two additional sections as a book

in 1986, after Blanchot published *La Communauté inavouable*, his response to Nancy's essay. For this history, see Morin, 72 ff. See also Ian James for contextualization of *La Communauté déoeuvrée* in relation to "the political" as articulated by Philippe Lacoue-Labarthe and Nancy at the Centre de Recherches Philosophiques sur le Politique during the years 1980–1984, 155 ff. See also Christopher Fynsk's introduction to Nancy's *Inoperative Community*.

2. For a lucid comparison of the concept of community in Agamben, Esposito, and Nancy, see the illuminating work of Greg Bird. See also Esposito, *Communitas*.

3. Giorgio Agamben, *The Coming Community*, 68.

4. Aristotle, *Nichomachean Ethics*, trans. Christopher Rowe, as quoted by Agamben, 5.

5. Zone Books, New York, 2009.

6. Kant's use of the term *sensus communis* deserves mention here. Kant seems to use the term to signify both an "inner sense" that is generated by the connection among the senses (para. 20, *Kritik der Urteilskraft*); and to mean a "sense" common to all humans equivalent to what he calls *Geschmack* (para. 40). Zhengi Zhouhuang describes this as the "intrasubjective" and "intersubjective" uses of the term. He writes: "Obwohl das Prinzip des Gemeinsinns im intrasubjektiven Sinne nur eine Wiederholung der Wirkung der subjektiven Zweckmäßigkeit ist, funktioniert es im intersubjektiven Sinne doch als ein normatives Prinzip" (96) ("Although the principle of common sense in the intrasubjective sense is only a repetition of the effect of subjective purposiveness, in the intersubjective sense, it nevertheless functions as a normative principle") (my translation). Jean-François Lyotard describes the *sensus communis* as a musical principle: "On dit toujours que le temps, sens interne, est l'auto-affection du sujet. Mais le *sensus* sentimental pur est une auto-affection encore plus pure, une espèce de cœnesthésie transcendantale, qui 'précède' toute mise en diachronie. Les accords ne s'organisent en ligne mélodique que secondairement, par organization du rythme dans le temps diachronique" (77) ("One always says that time, an inner sense, is the auto-affection of the subject. But the pure sentimental *sensus* is an even more pure self-affection, a kind of transcendental cœnesthesia, that precedes all diachrony. Chords are organized in a melodic line only secondarily by the organization of rhythm in diachronic time") (my translation). *Sensus communis* is a "principe d'unification, mais plutôt d'unisson, des diverses voix facultaires" (82) ("principle of unification, or sooner of unison, of the voices of the diverse faculties") (my translation). Jan Mieszkowski demonstrates the dual nature of *sensus communis* as a principle that both unites and separates: "The 'common sense' that for Kant makes us all human is not merely a force of joining or uniting, whether as a synthesis that constructs concepts or as a gathering of people's opinions. *Sensus communis* is as much an impetus for a retreat into parts as it is a connection of one person or concept with another person or concept" (298, in Payne and Thorpe, *Kant and the Concept of Community*). See Ritter and Gründer, *Historisches Wörterbuch der Philosophie*, vol. 9, 622–79. To my knowledge, Kant does not use the term *synaesthesia*.

7. See *Aesthetik* II, 254–55: smell, taste, and touch are excluded from the realm of art, which is divided between the visual and the auditory.

8. Jean-Luc Nancy, *Les Muses* (Paris: Editions Galilée, 1994), *The Muses*, trans. Peggy Kamuf (Stanford: Stanford University Press, 1996).

9. In *Phenomenology of Perception*, Merleau-Ponty describes "normal" perception as a kind of synaesthesia: "The senses intercommunicate by opening on to the structure of the thing. One sees the hardness and brittleness of glass, and when, with a tinkling sound, it breaks, this sound is conveyed by the visible glass. One sees the springiness of steel, the ductility of red-hot steel, the hardness of a plane blade, the softness of shavings. The form of objects is not their geometrical shape: it stands in a certain relation to their specific nature, and appeals to all our other senses as well as sight" (267).

10. Jacques Derrida has elaborated on the importance of touch for Nancy in his book *Le Toucher, On Touching—Jean-Luc Nancy*. He criticizes Nancy's play on the word *touch* and its double valence: "Nancy seems to be drawing on the fund of an old rhetoric that says 'to touch' for 'to concern,' 'to aim,' to think,' 'to refer to,' 'to speak of,' 'to take as its object,' 'to thematize' precisely, and so forth. . . . Nancy plays this game—the most serious game there is—which consists in using, as if there were not the slightest problem, this common and ancestral figure of tactile language in order to draw our attention to 'touch' itself and to this invasion that, little by little, prevents us from distinguishing between the thematic meaning and operative function, between the proper or literal sense of this sense and all its tropic turns of phrase" (268).

11. Jonathan Culler, "Intertextuality and Interpretation: Baudelaire's 'Correspondances,'" in *Nineteenth-century French Poetry: Introductions to Close Readings*, ed. Christopher Prendergast (Cambridge: Cambridge University Press, 1990), 120.

12. Theodor W. Adorno, "Die Kunst und die Künste," in *"Ob nach Auschwitz noch sich leben lasse": Ein philosophisches Lesebuch*, ed. Rolf Tiedemann (Leipzig: Edition Suhrkamp, 1997), 426.

13. For a thorough treatment of "constellation," see Andrea Krauß, *Lenz unter anderem*. See also her introduction to *Constellations/Konstellationen*.

14. In *the Logic of Sensation*, Deleuze discusses the unity of the arts in terms of Rhythm, written with a capital *R*. He writes: "The painter would thus *make visible* a kind of original unity of the senses, and would make a multisensible Figure appear visually. But this operation is possible only if the sensation of a particular domain (here, the visual sensation) is in direct contact with a vital power that exceeds every domain and traverses them all. This power is Rhythm, which is more profound than vision, hearing, etc." *The Logic of Sensation*, trans. Daniel W. Smith (Minneapolis: University of Minnesota Press, 2003, 37.

15. Theodor W. Adorno, *Gesammelte Schriften*, ed. Rolf Tiedemann (Frankfurt am Main: Suhrkamp, 1978), 16: 634.

Chapter 2

1. Franz Liszt, *An Artist's Journey*, 94.

2. Sachs: "The supernatural, ghostly sound of these chords, changing, increasing and fading away with the wind without any player or any artificial contrivance, was wholly romantic. Between 1780 and 1860, therefore, aeolian harps were much in favor in parks, on roofs and on ruins of medieval castles, especially in Germany and England" (402).

3. M. H. Abrams, *The Correspondent Breeze*, 26.

4. See the entry, "Aeolian Harp," in *The New Grove Encyclopedia of Music*, 1: 173–75; Geoffrey Grigson, *The Harp of Aeolus* (London: Routledge, 1947), 24–31; Curt Sachs, *The History of Musical Instruments* (New York: Norton, 1940), 402.

5. *Grove*, 619.

6. Thompson's poems are treated as precursors to Coleridge's by James H. Averill in "Coleridge's 'The Eolian Harp' and James Thomson's 'An Ode on Aeolus's Harp.'" *English Language Notes* 16 (1979): 223–27. For more historical genealogy, see C. G. Martin, "Coleridge and Cudworth: A Source for 'The Eolian Harp,'" *Notes and Queries* (1966), 13: 173–76.

7. See Rameau, Jean-Philippe. "Traité de l'Harmonie reduite à ses Principes Naturels." *Complete Theoretical Writings*, vol. 1. Ed. Erwin R. Jacobi (American Institute of Musicology, 1967); and Jean le Rond d'Alembert, "Discours Préliminaire de l'Encyclopédie," *Oeuvres Complètes*, vol. 2 (Paris, 1821), 17–99; and *Elemens de Musique theorique et pratique* (New York: Boude Brothers, 1966). Chladni published his research on "Die Akustik" on the velocity of the transmission of sound through solid bodies in 1802. This research generated the phenomenon of "Chladni figures," or in German *Klangfiguren*. Chladni's text includes popularized instructions, apparently suitable for the home, about how to set up a metal plate and transmit tones to produce the corresponding figures in sand. The interest in technological games connected with sound and strings takes place contemporaneously with developments of automata, including Vaucanson's famous flute-player and other musical automata in France, as well as phenomena of electricity. Magnetism, too, becomes a parlor game around the same time. For thorough historical treatments of these sciences and their relationship to music, see Weliver and Jamie C. Kassler, *Music, Science, Philosophy* (Aldershot: Ashgate, 2001).

8. Grigson points this out but doesn't make much of the contradiction: "Man, by artifice, if not art, arranges several strings on a rectangular pine-wood box, the wind moves the strings; and the man-arranged music is not man-made, but made from Nature, is Nature's music, made audible. A self-deception, but how useful in image, how delightful a toy for the next seventy years!" (29).

9. E. T. A. Hoffmann, *The Best Tales of Hoffmann* (New York: Dover, 1967), 98. The passage is from the story, "Die Automate." The German text reads: "Kann denn . . . die Musik, die in unserm Innern wohnt, eine andere sein als die, welche in

der Natur wie ein tiefes, nur dem höhern Sinn erforschliches Geheimnis verborgen, und die durch das Organ der Instrumente nur wie im Zwange eines mächtigen Zaubers, dessen wir Herr worden, ertönt?" Die Serapionsbrüder. (Frankfurt am Main: Insel Verlag, 1983), 2: 463.

10. " 'Aber im reinpsychischen Wirken des Geistes, im Traume ist der Bann gelöst, und wir hören selbst im Konzert bekannter Instrumente jene Naturlaute, wie sie wunderbar, in der Luft erzeugt, auf uns niederschweben, anschwellen und verhallen.' 'Ich denke an die Äolsharfe,' unterbrach Ferdinand," 2: 463.

11. "Wenn sie den Gesang in einfachen Melismen bald in die Höhe führte, daß die Töne wie helle Kristallglocken erklangen, bald in die Tiefe hinabsenkte, daß er in den dumpfen Seufzern einer hoffnungslosen Klage zu ersterben schien, dann fühlte ich, wie ein unnennbares Entzücken mein Innerstes durchbebte, wie der Schmerz der unendlichen Sehnsucht meine Brust krampfhaft zusammenzog, wie mein Atem stockte, wie mein Selbst unterging in namenloser, himmlischer Wollust. Ich wagte nicht, mich zu regen, meine ganze Seele, mein ganzes Gemüt war nur Ohr," 2: 443.

12. The notion of existence as spasm is important in Avital Ronell's analysis of epilepsy, poetic language, and irony in *Stupidity* (Urbana: University of Illinois Press, 2002).

13. See Kimio Ogawa (in Weliver) for a detailed comparison of the medical discourse on nerves in relation to musical instruments. I have analyzed a similar figure in Baudelaire in *Virtuosity of the Nineteenth Century*, especially in chapter 8, "Music, Painting and Writing in Baudelaire's *Petits poëmes en prose*."

14. Baudelaire, for example, quotes Hoffmann's Kreisleriana in his Salons de 1846 to illustrate the principle of synaesthesia. See E. T. A. Hoffmann, "Höchst zerstreute Gedanken," in *Kreisleriana* (Stuttgart: Reclam, 1983), 39–40, and Charles Baudelaire, *Oeuvres Complètes* (Paris: Bibliothèque de la Pléiade: 1975), vol. 2, 425–26.

15. See Sigmund Freud's essay, "Das Unheimliche," in which Freud analyzes Hoffmann's story, "The Sandman."

Chapter 3

1. My presentation here reiterates the impeccable reading of Barbara Johnson in "Poetry and Its Double: Two *Invitations au Voyage*" in *The Critical Difference*. Specifically, she stresses the reversibility between the "fleur incomparable," as the unique poetic word, and its substitutability (31). Mary Ann Caws also expresses the "ready-made" quality of the black tulip and the blue dahlia (32). Doyle Calhoun argues that the creation of allegory through the violent transplantation of an image into poetry is grounded in contemporary practices of urban botany.

2. Elissa Marder, "Baudelaire's Bad Sex," *differences* 27, no. 1 (2016): 3.

3. Paul de Man suggests that the "forêt de symboles" can be read as a "foule de symboles," connecting it to the prosaic world of the modern city. Likewise, he reminds us that *correspondance* also names transfer tickets on modern transit systems, pointing to the way in which the sonnet tends to undo itself. "Anthropomorphism and Trope in the Lyric," 246 and 251. Beryl Schlossman also reads *correspondance* as a disseminating force intimately connected to the city in "Benjamin's 'Über einige Motive bei Baudelaire': The Secret Architecture of Correspondances."

4. In *The Dream of an Absolute Language*, Lynn R. Wilkinson questions how much Baudelaire had actually read Swedenborg. She writes instead of a "Swedenborgianism," that is, a discursive formation of both elite and popular culture in the nineteenth century. She tracks all of the occurrences of the word *correspondance(s)* and *Swedenborg* in Baudelaire's works, finding seven and eight, respectively, in Baudelaire's prose, and one occurrence of *correspondance* in the poem of that name, and no instances of "*Swedenborg*" in the poetry. Devin P. Zuber makes out Baudelaire's connection to Swedenborg to be more intense in *A Language of Things* (63), in which he tries to rehabilitate Swedenborg for contemporary environmental interests.

5. Cf. the following fragment in *Das Passagen-Werk*: "Zwischen der Theorie der natürlichen Korrespondenzen und der Absage an die Natur besteht ein Widerspruch. Er löst sich auf, indem die Impressionen in der Erinnerung vom Erlebnis entbunden werden, so daß die in ihnen gebundene Erfahrung frei wird und zum allegorischen Fundus geschlagen werden kann" (*PW* J, 66, 5, vol. 1: 436).

6. In his insightful and often cited book, *Baudelaire and Freud*, Leo Bersani breaks up the so-called vertical correspondences of the first stanza of the poem in its turn to the "horizontal unity" of synaesthesia in the following stanzas (32–33). Bersani reads a metaphysical dimension of correspondence (between word and nature) in the first and final stanzas, which is resisted by the "infinite expansion" of the "*parfums*" outlined in the poem. His reading foreshadows Paul de Man's now-famous reading of the dislocated status of the simile word *comme*. Eugene Holland hails "Correspondances" as the embodiment of Baudelaire's aesthetics understood as a romantic symbolism, and continues: "But romanticism was a stance Baudelaire came to regard with suspicion, even disdain. Far from being the key to *Les Fleurs du Mal*, "Correspondances" epitomizes an aesthetic that the rest of the collection will work to undermine and ultimately reject" (43). At the same time, he sees a tendency of "Correspondances" to undermine itself in the stanzas about infinite expansion. "My claim," he writes, "is rather that, regardless of and perhaps even sometimes against Baudelaire's conscious intentions and most trenchant declarations, his most characteristically modern poetry registers a trajectory away from the metaphoricity of romantic symbolism, via its decoding by a metonymic poetics. This metonymic poetics . . . is already at work in the verse collection, as we have seen . . . [there is a] tension between the semantics and poetics, between metaphor and metonymy, between a romanticism being abandoned and a modernism still in the making. Indeed, it would be possible retrospectively to reread even 'Correspondances' itself

in light of such a tension: not (as it has most often been read, and as I reiterated at the beginning of the chapter) as crystallizing the aesthetic program of romantic symbolism, but rather as already prefiguring the move away from it" (76).

7. See Gordon, *Synaesthetics—Art as Synaesthesia*, 51–73.

8. See Jonathan Culler, "Intertextuality and Interpretation: Baudelaire's 'Correspondances,'" esp. 119–20.

9. Kevin McLaughlin discusses this oscillation insightfully in his chapter, "Poetic Reason of State: Baudelaire and the Multitudes" in *Poetic Force*.

10. 266; see also McLaughlin's remarks on "philological community," xx–xxi. Cf. Werner Hamacher, "Für—die Philologie."

11. Lacoue-Labarthe discusses how Baudelaire finds himself in Wagner's music. See the opening pages of *Musica Ficta*.

12. I have discussed these relationships at length in *Virtuosity of the Nineteenth-Century*.

13. Benjamin notes this in "Über einige Motive bei Baudelaire." McLaughlin illuminates the concept of "reason of state" in *Poetic Force*, 55–58.

14. As Paul de Man has argued, the double valence of the term *comme* confuses this unifying simile with the uncontrolled numerical expansion of terms in the final stanza. The latter *comme* opens up a potentially infinite series of singularities that cannot be gathered together, and begin to enact the "expansion des choses infinies" opened up in the poem. Cf. "Anthropomorphism and Trope," 249.

15. De Man also comments on the incongruity of the "green" simile, as well as the troubled simile of "Vaste comme la nuit et comme la clarté," 248.

16. Here I'll just gesture at the similar structure of the neighboring poem, "Un Fantôme." In that poem, the speaker says explicitly: "I am like a painter," and the sections are names, "The Darkness, Perfume, The Frame, and the Portrait." "Je suis comme un peintre"—the sections are named "Les Ténèbres, Le Parfum, Le Cadre and Le Portrait."

17. De Man reads "Obsession" as the romantic lyric counterpart to "Correspondances."

18. There is an editorial suggestion that this quatrain was composed later than the others and added.

19. Jennifer Phillips also allies this paragraph of "De la Couleur" with *correspondances* thought of as a dynamic process rather than a fixed set of meanings: "Baudelaire's vision of color serves to remind us that *correspondance* is not a fixed, one-to-one comparison, but rather a process—a dynamic flow and exchange of characteristics, a relay of identifications that are neither linear nor static, a suppression of autonomy in favor of reciprocity." "Relative Color," 349.

20. Phillips reads this as the interaction between originality and cliché, tending almost to plagiarism, in the *Salon de 1846*. She points also to the multiplicity of the critical voice in the essay. See "'Vox populi, vox dei': Baudelaire's Uncommon Use of Commonplace in the Salon de 1846."

Chapter 4

1. Richard Wagner, "Art and Revolution," in *The Artwork of the Future and Other Works*, 34–35.
2. Hence Nietzsche's "In Formel: Wagner und Liszt." See my essay, "In Formel: 'Wagner und Liszt.'"
3. Friedrich Nietzsche, "Unzeitgemäße Betrachtungen," in *Kritische Studienausgabe*, 1: 466, 485.
4. Friedrich Nietzsche, *Untimely Meditations*, 222 and 236.
5. In *Musica Ficta*, Lacoue-Labarthe quotes Heidegger on the importance of Nietzsche's views on Wagner to the history of philosophy: "'Nietzsche's antagonism to Wagner becomes comprehensible as the necessary turning point of our history'" (88). For a contrary reading of the importance of Wagner for philosophy, see also Alain Badiou, *Five Lessons on Wagner*.
6. Karol Berger, *Beyond Reason*, 375. Berger dates Nietzsche's real break with Wagner to 1878.
7. See also Jean-Luc Nancy, *Le Partage des voix* on partitioning, performance, and interpretation.
8. See Philippe Lacoue-Labarthe, *L'Imitation des modernes*.
9. Immanuel Kant, *Kritik der Urteilskraft*, 131 (para. 9, "Untersuchung der Frage").

Chapter 5

1. Françoise Meltzer, *Salome and the Dance of Writing*, 21. Murray Krieger, *Ekphrasis*.
2. This point is also made by James A. W. Heffernan, *Museum of Words*.
3. For everything you ever wanted to know about smell and representation, see Rindisbacher, *The Smell of Books*
4. For Freud on smell, see *Gesammelte Schriften* VIII, 90; XIV, 458, 466.
5. Joris-Karl Huysmans, *Against Nature*, 51. *À Rebours*, 146–47.
6. Peter Cooke, *Gustave Moreau*, 82.
7. Cooke reads this in a contrary way, writing of Moreau's Salome: "In this way, in keeping with the traditional ideals of history painting, Moreau was able to emphasise the timeless universality of his subject, which, in his eyes, represented 'la femme éternelle,'" in "'It Isn't a Dance,'" 222. Natasha Grigorian similarly argues that, despite the seeming similarity between Huysmans and Moreau, for the painter, Salome maintains a transcendent symbolic role, while Huysmans/des Esseintes is more in tune with the "monstrous beauty" of the figure. Both Cooke and Grigorian stress that Moreau's aesthetic is more linked to that of traditional history painting, while that of Huysmans points forward from naturalism to symbolism.

8. Meltzer, 25. Meltzer provides an excellent summary and analysis of the biblical background to the story of Salome. For a succinct account of the Salome story and its representations, see also Dimova, "Decadent Senses."
9. Stéphane Mallarmé, *Hérodiade*, trans. David Lenson. *Oeuvres Complètes*.
10. See Peter Szondi, *Poésies et Poétiques de la modernité*, 88.

Chapter 6

1. For focused discussions of the truth in Heidegger, see Taylor Carmen and Mark A. Wrathall. Neither Carmen nor Wrathall considers the term *Entsprechung* in relation to correspondence.
2. In "Anthropomorphism and Trope," Paul de Man remarks that the sonnet is "canonical and programmatic" (243). For elucidating readings of the sonnet, see Jonathan Culler, "Intertextuality and Interpretation: Baudelaire's 'Corresondances' "; Walter Benjamin, "Über einige Motive bei Baudelaire," *Gesammelte Schriften*, vol. 1.2; and Beryl Schlossman. Culler and Schlossman both provide ample bibliography of the sources and context of correspondence. For a very thorough intellectual history, see Wilkinson.
3. I am indebted to Jacques Derrida, *Politiques de l'amitié*, for drawing my attention to this text. See especially pp. 367 ff. For a riveting account of Heidegger's visit to France, see Ethan Kleinberg, *Generation Existential*, 199–206.
4. Martin Heidegger, *Sein und Zeit*, 219. Further page references will be incorporated parenthetically. The first number refers to the German edition, the second to the English translation.
5. On the relation of the concept of truth as correspondence and the status of propositional truth, see *Die Geschichte des philosophischen Begriffs der Wahrheit*, and *La vérité—Antiquité—Modernité*.
6. Martin Heidegger, *Wegmarken*, 181.
7. Martin Heidegger, *What Is Philosophy?* 44–45. Françoise Dastur comments on this passage in her elucidating essay, "Heidegger and the Question of the 'Essence' of Language," 233.
8. Heidegger articulates the "fall" into Latin for example in *Der Ursprung des Kunstwerkes* (*The Origin of the Work of Art*): "Diese Übersetzung der griechischen Namen in die lateinische Sprache ist keineswegs der folgenlose Vorgang, für den er noch heutigentags gehalten wird. Vielmehr verbirgt sich hinter der anscheinend wörtlich und somit bewahrenden Übersetzung ein *Über*setzen griechsischer Erfahrung in eine andere Denkungsart. *Das römische Denken übernimmt die griechischen Wörter ohne die entsprechende gleichursprüngliche Erfahrung dessen, was sie sagen, ohne das griechische Wort*. Die Bodenlosigkeit des abendländischen Denkens beginnt mit diesem Übersetzen." *Holzwege* 7 ("However, this translation of Greek names into Latin is in no way the innocent process it is considered to this day. Beneath the seemingly

literal and thus faithful translation there is concealed, rather, a *translation of Greek experience into a different way of thinking. Roman thought takes over the Greek words without a corresponding, equally authentic experience of what they say, without the Greek word.* The rootlessness of Western thought begins with this translation." *Poetry, Language, Thought*), 23.

    9. On Heidegger's reading of Plato I am indebted to Howard Eiland, "The Pedagogy of Shadow: Heidegger and Plato"; Partenie and Rockmore, *Heidegger and Plato: Toward Dialogue;* and Francisco J. Gonzalez, *Plato and Heidegger: A Question of Dialogue.*

    10. Martin Heidegger, *Wegmarken*, 228–29.

    11. Martin Heidegger, *Pathmarks*, 177.

    12. In this context, scholars regularly cite Heidegger's apparent reversal of the hypothesis of a "Wesenswandel" of truth in Plato in "Das Ende der Philosophie und die Aufgabe des Denkens" in *Zur Sache des Denkens*. Here I am not so much concerned with Heidegger's interpretation of Plato as with the analyses of unconcealedness and correctness. In "Das Ende," Heidegger dissociates the two: "In jedem Fall wird das eine klar: Die Frage nach der Αληθεια, nach der Unverborgenheit als solcher, ist nicht die Frage nach der Wahrheit. Darum war es nicht sachgemäss und demzufolge irreführend, die Αληθεια im Sinne der Lichtung Wahrheit zu nennen.... Im Gesichtskreis dieser Frage muss anerkannt werden, dass die Αληθεια, die Unverborgenheit im Sinne der Lichtung von Anwesenheit sogleich und nur als ορθοτης, als die Richtigkeit des Vorstellens und Aussagens erfahren wurde. Dann ist aber auch die Behauptung von einem Wesenswandel der Wahrheit, d.h. von der Unverborgenheit zur Richtigkeit, nicht haltbar" (77–78) ("In any case, one thing is clear: the question about Αληθεια, about unconcealedness as such, is not the question about Truth. Therefore it was not correct and thus misleading to call Αληθεια, in the sense of the clearing, the Truth.... In the circle of this question, it must be acknowledged that Αληθεια, unconcealedness, in the sense of the clearing of presence, was experienced at the same time and only as ορθοτης, as correctness of representation and enunciation. But then the claim of an essential turn of truth, that is, of unconcealedness to correctness, is untenable") (my translation).

    13. Interestingly, the *Oxford English Dictionary* defines *converse* as "to pass one's life, live, dwell in or with, in modern French also to exchange words with; = Provençal *conversar*, Spanish *conversar*, Italian and late Latin *conversare* < Latin *conversārī* lit. to turn oneself about, to move to and fro, pass one's life, dwell, abide, live somewhere, keep company with." This would be very much in line with Heidegger's equation of *entsprechen* and *wohnen* in "Dichterisch wohnet der Mensch."

    14. The terms *vertical* and *horizontal* recall Roman Jakobson's famous designations of the axes of metaphor and metonymy. Claude Pichois, editor of the Pléiade edition of Baudelaire, writes that the vertical characterizes correspondences, while the horizontal qualifies the relation among the senses of synaesthesia: "De tradition, on distingue, en effet, les corresondances des synesthésies. Les premières sont verticals et

irréversibles: elles orientent l'homme vers Dieu selon les degrés hiérachiques d'une spiritualization. À cet égard, elles constituent bien une mystique, au sens strict, c'est-à-dire une methode, une technique qui permet à l'homme de s'unir immédiatement à Dieu, à la creature de se fondre dans l'Incréé. Les synesthésies . . . sont horizontals, faisant communiquer les sens entre eux; elles sont reversible: un son peut aussi bien provoquer une image colorée qu'être provoqué par elle." Charles Baudelaire, *Oeuvres Complètes*, ed. Claude Pichoid, 843 ("Traditionally, in fact, the correspondences are distinguished from synaesthesias. The former are vertical and irreversible: they orient man toward God according to the hierarchical degrees of a spiritualization. In this regard, they do constitute a mysticism in the strict sense, that is to say, a method, a technique that allows man to be immediately unified with God, allows the creature to merge with the Uncreated. The synaesthesias . . . are horizontal, making the senses communicate among themselves; they are reversible: a sound can just as well provoke an image as be provoked by it") (my translation). See also Claude Pichois and Jean-Paul Avice, *Dictionnaire Baudelaire*, 128.

15. See the *Oxford English Dictionary* on "discussion": "Latin *discuss-* participial stem of *discut-ĕre* to dash or shake to pieces, agitate, disperse, dispel, drive away."

16. Gerhard Richter provides an interesting gloss on the verb *entsprechen* in *Afterness*, 102–3. While he points to the many ways one could and should translate *entsprechen*, my point here is that Heidegger forecloses this possibility by supplying the French term *correspondance* so emphatically, thus invoking a certain context that would be familiar to readers of French in 1955.

17. Derrida discusses this comment in *Heidegger et la Question*, 87.

18. Martin Heidegger, *Heraklit, Gesamtausgabe*, 55, 250.

19. Martin Heidegger, *Unterwegs zur Sprache*, 32–33.

20. Martin Heidegger, *Poetry, Language, Thought*, 207.

21. Werner Hamacher, *Für—die philologie*, 70; *Minima Philologica*, 150.

22. Werner Hamacher, *für—die philologie*, 69–70.

23. Quoted in Pichois and Avice, 129.

A Note on Rhythm

1. For readings of this kind, see Henri Lefebvre, *rhythmanalysis*, and Caroline Levine, *Forms*.

Bibliography

Adorno, Theodor W. *Can One Live after Auschwitz? A Philosophical Reader.* Ed. Rolf Tiedemann. Stanford, CA: Stanford University Press, 2003.

———. "Die Kunst und die Künste," in *"Ob nach Auschwitz noch sich leben lasse": Ein philosophisches Lesebuch.* Ed. Rolf Tiedemann. Leipzig, Germany: Suhrkamp Verlag, 1997.

———. *Gesammelte Schriften.* Ed. Rolf Tiedemann. Frankfurt am Main, Germany: Suhrkamp Verlag, 1978.

———. *Negative Dialectics.* Trans. E. B. Ashton. London: Routledge, 1973.

———. *Negative Dialektik: Jargon der Eigentlichkeit.* Frankfurt am Main, Germany: Suhrkamp Verlag, 1970.

———. "On Some Relations between Music and Painting." Trans. Susan Gillespie. *The Musical Quarterly* 70, no. 1 (Spring 1995): 66–79.

Agamben, Giorgio. *The Coming Community.* Trans. Michael Hardt. Minneapolis: University of Minnesota Press, 1993.

———. "Friendship." Trans. Joseph Falsone. *Contretemps* 5 (December 2004), 2–7.

Antosh, Ruth B. *Reality and Illusion in the Novels of J.-K. Huysmans.* Amsterdam: Rodopi, 1986.

———. "The Role of Painting in Three Novels by J.-K. Huysmans. *Nineteenth-Century French Studies* 12/13, no. 4/1 (1984): 131–46.

Aristotle. *Nichomachean Ethics.* Trans. Christopher Rowe. Oxford, UK: Oxford University Press, 2002.

Badiou, Alain. *Five Lessons on Wagner.* Trans. Susan Spitzer. London: Verso, 2010.

Baudelaire, Charles. *Art in Paris 1845–1862—Salons and Other Exhibitions Reviewed by Charles Baudelaire.* Trans. Jonathan Mayne. Ithaca, NY: Cornell University Press, 1965.

———. *The Flowers of Evil.* Trans. Keith Waldrop. Middletown, CT: Wesleyan University Press, 2006.

———. *Œuvres complètes.* 2 vols. Ed. Claude Pichois. Paris: Gallimard, 1975.

———. *The Painter of Modern Life and Other Essays.* Trans. Jonathan Mayne. London: Phaidon, 1995.

———. *Paris Spleen: Little Poems in Prose*. Trans. Keith Waldrop. Middletown, CT: Wesleyan University Press, 2009.
Baron-Cohen, Simon, and John E. Harrison. *Synaesthesia: Classic and Contemporary Readings*. Oxford, UK: Blackwell Publishers, 1997.
Benjamin, Walter. *The Arcades Project*. Trans. Howard Eiland and Kevin McLaughlin. Cambridge, MA: Harvard University Press, 1999.
———. *Das Passagen-Werk*. Ed. Rolf Tiedemann. Frankfurt am Main, Germany: Suhrkamp, 1982.
———. *Gesammelte Schriften*. Ed. Rolf Tiedemann and Hermann Schweppenhäuser. Frankfurt am Main, Germany: Suhrkamp Taschenbuch Verlag, 1991.
———. *The Origin of German Tragic Drama*. Trans. John Osborne. London: Verso, 1977.
———. *Selected Writings, Vol. 4: 1938–1940*. Ed. Howard Eiland and Michael W. Jennings. Cambridge, MA: Harvard University Press, 2003.
Benveniste, Emile. *Problems in General Linguistics*. Coral Gables, FL: University of Miami Press, 1971.
Berger, Karol. *Beyond Reason: Wagner contra Nietzsche*. Berkeley and Los Angeles: University of California Press, 2017.
Bernstein, Susan. "In Formel: 'Wagner und Liszt.'" *New German Critique* (October 1996): 85–97.
———. *Virtuosity of the Nineteenth Century: Performing Music and Language in Heine, Liszt, and Baudelaire*. Stanford, CA: Stanford University Press, 1989.
Bersani, Leo. *Baudelaire and Freud*. Berkeley and Los Angeles: University of California Press, 1977.
Bird, Greg. *Containing Community: From Political Economy to Ontology in Agamben, Esposito, and Nancy*. Albany: State University of New York Press, 2016.
Blanchot, Maurice. *La Communauté inavouable*. Paris: Les Editions de Minuit, 1983.
Braswell, Suzanne. "Mallarmé, Huysmans, and the Poetics of Hothouse Blooms." *French Forum* 38, no. 1/2 (Winter/Spring 2013): 69–87.
Brill, Sara. *Aristotle on the Concept of Shared Life*. Oxford, UK: Oxford University Press, 2020.
Bucknell, Brad. "On 'Seeing' Salome." *ELH* 60, no. 2 (1993): 503–26.
Calhoun, Doyle. "Flowers for Baudelaire: Urban Botany and Allegorical Writing." *Nineteenth-Century French Studies* 49, nos. 1–2 (Fall–Winter 2020–21): 17–34.
Cavallaro, Dani. *Synesthesia and the Arts*. Jefferson, North Carolina: McFarland, 2013.
Caws, Mary Ann. "Decentering the Invitation, to Take the Trip." *L'Esprit Créateur* 34, no. 3 (Fall 1994): 28–34.
Claviez, Thomas, ed. Foreword Jean-Luc Nancy. *The Common Growl: Toward a Poetics of Precarious Community*. New York: Fordham University Press, 2016.
Cohn, Robert Greer, ed. *Mallarmé in the Twentieth Century*. Cranbury, NJ: Associated University Presses, 1998.

Cooke, Peter. *Gustave Moreau: History Painting, Spirituality and Symbolism.* New Haven, CT: Yale University Press, 2014.

———. "'It Isn't a Dance': Gustave Moreau's 'Salome' and 'The Apparition.'" *Dance Research: Journal of the Society for Dance Research* 29, no. 2 (Winter 2011), 214–32.

———. "Symbolism, Decadence and Gustave Moreau." *Burlington Magazine* 151, no. 1274 (May 2009): 312–18.

Culler, Jonathan. "Intertextuality and Interpretation: Baudelaire's 'Correspondances.'" *Nineteenth-century French Poetry: Introductions to Close Reading.* Ed. Christopher Prendergast. Cambridge, UK: Cambridge University Press, 1990.

Cytowic, Richard E. *Synesthesia: A Union of the Senses.* Cambridge, MA: MIT Press, 2002.

Cytowic, Richard E., and David M. Eagleman. *Wednesday Is Indigo Blue: Discovering the Brain of Synaesthesia.* Cambridge, MA: MIT Press, 2009.

Dann, Kevin T. *Bright Colors Falsely Seen: Synaesthesia and the Search for Transcendental Knowledge.* New Haven and London: Yale University Press, 1998.

Deleuze, Gilles. *The Logic of Sensation.* Trans. Daniel W. Smith. Minneapolis: University of Minnesota Press, 2003.

De Man, Paul. *Allegories of Reading: Figural Language in Rousseau, Nietzsche, Rilke, and Proust.* New Haven, CT: Yale University Press, 1979.

———. "Anthropomorphism and Trope in the Lyric." *The Rhetoric of Romanticism.* New York: Columbia University Press, 1984.

Derrida, Jacques. *Margins of Philosophy.* Trans. Alan Bass. Chicago, IL: University of Chicago Press, 1992.

———. "*Le Toucher*—Touch/to touch him." *Paragraph* 16, no. 2 (1993): 131–32.

Dejanovic, Sanja, ed. *Nancy and the Political.* Edinburgh, UK: Edinburgh University Press, 2015.

Devisch, Ignaas. *Jean-Luc Nancy and the Question of Community.* London: Bloomsbury, 2011.

Dimova, Polina. "Decadent Senses: The Dissemination of Oscar Wilde's *Salome* across the Arts." *Performing Salome, Revealing Stories.* Ed. Claire Rowden. Farnham, UK: Ashgate, 2013, 15–47.

———. "Synaesthesia." *The Routledge Encyclopedia of Modernism.* Routledge: 2016.

Eiland, Howard. "The Pedagogy of Shadow: Heidegger and Plato." *boundary 2*, 16, no. 2/3 (Winter–Spring 1989): 13–39.

Freud, Sigmund. *Gesammelte Werke.* Frankfurt am Main, Germany: Fischer Taschenbuch Verlag, 1999.

Gasché, Rodolphe. "The Falls of History: Huysmans's *A Rebours. Yale French Studies* 74 (1988): 183–204.

Gonzalez, Francisco J. *Plato and Heidegger: A Question of Dialogue.* University Park: Pennsylvania State University Press, 2009.

Gordon, Paul. *Synaesthetics: Art as Synaesthesia*. London: Bloomsbury, 2020.
Grigorian, Natasha. "The Writings of J.-K. Huysmans and Gustave Moreau's Painting: Affinity or Divergence?" *Nineteenth-Century French Studies* 32, no. 3/4 (Spring–Summer 2004): 282–97.
Hamacher, Werner. *Für—die Philologie*. Frankfurt am Main, Germany: roughradio, 2009.
———. *Minima Philologica*. Trans. Catherine Diehl and Jason Groves. New York: Fordham University Press, 2015.
Hansche, Rainer J. "Nietzsche's Synaesthetic Epistemology and the Restitution of the Holistic Human." In *Nietzsche and the Becoming of Life*, Ed. Vanessa Lemm. New York: Fordham University Press, 2015, 343–48.
Heffernan, James A. W. *Museum of Words: The Poetics of Ekphrasis from Homer to Ashbery*. Chicago, IL: University of Chicago Press, 1993.
Heidegger, Martin. *Being and Time*. Trans. John Macquarrie and Edward Robinson. New York: Harper & Row, 1962.
———. *Gesamtausgabe*, vol. 55. *Herklit*. Frankfurt am Main, Germany: Vittorio Klostermann, 1979.
———. *Heraclitus: The Inception of Occidental Thinking; Logic: Heraclitus's Doctrine of the Logos*. Trans. Julia Goesser Assaiante and S. Montgomery Ewegen. London: Bloomsbury, 2018.
———. *Holzwege*. Frankfurt am Main, Germany: Vittorio Klostermann, 1950.
———. *Pathmarks*. Ed. William McNeill. Cambridge, UK: Cambridge University Press, 1998.
———. *Poetry, Language, Thought*. Trans. Albert Hofstadter. New York: Harper and Row, 1971.
———. *Sein und Zeit*. Tübingen, Germany: Max Niemeyer Verlag, 1977.
———. *Unterwegs zur Sprache*. Stuttgart, Germany: Verlag Günther Neske, 1959.
———. *Wegmarken*. Frankfurt am Main, Germany: Vittorio Klostermann, 1978.
———. *What Is Philosophy?* Bilingual ed. Trans. William Kluback and Jean T. Wilde. London: Vision Press, 1958.
———. *Zur Sache des Denkens*. Tübingen, Germany: Max Niemeyer Verlag, 1969.
Heller-Roazen, Daniel. *The Inner Touch: Archaeology of a Sensation*. New York: Zone Books, 2009.
Hoffmann, Benjamin. "L'Esthétique de la Condensation chez Villiers, Huysmans et Mallarmé." *Etudes Stéphane Mallarmé* 4 (2016): 63–76.
Holland, Eugene W. *Baudelaire and Schizoanalysis: The Sociopoetics of Modernism*. Cambridge, UK: Cambridge University Press, 1993.
Huysmans, Joris-Karl. *Against Nature*. Trans. Robert Baldick. Introduction and Notes Patrick McGuinness. London: Penguin Books, 2003.
———. *À Rebours*. Ed. Marc Fumaroli. Paris: Gallimard, 1977.
James, Ian. *The Fragmentary Demand: An Introduction to the Philosophy of Jean-Luc Nancy*. Stanford, CA: Stanford University Press, 2006.

Johnson, Barbara. *The Critical Difference: Essays in Contemporary Rhetoric of Reading.* Baltimore, MD: Johns Hopkins University Press, 1980.
Kandinsky, Wassily. *Concerning the Spiritual in Art.* Trans. M. T. H. Sadler. Dover: New York, 1977.
Kant, Immanuel. *Kritik der Urteilskraft.* Ed. Wilhelm Weischedel. Frankfurt am Main, Germany: Suhrkamp Verlag, 1981.
Kaplan, Julius. *The Art of Gustave Moreau: Theory, Style, and Content.* Ann Arbor, MI: UMI Research Press, 1982.
Krauß, Andrea. *Lenz unter anderem: Aspekte einer Theorie der Konstellation.* Zurich, Switzerland: Diaphanes, 2011.
Krieger, Murray. *Ekphrasis: The Illusion of the Natural Sign.* Baltimore, MD: Johns Hopkins University Press, 1992.
Lacoue-Labarthe, Philippe. *L'Imitation des modernes.* Paris: Editions Galilée, 1995.
———. *Musica Ficta (Figures de Wagner).* Paris: Christian Bourgois, 1991.
———. *Typography: Mimesis, Philosophy, Politics.* Ed. Christopher Fynsk. Stanford. CA: Stanford University Press, 1989.
Lefebvre, Henri. *Rhythmanalysis: Space, Time and Everyday Life.* Trans. Stuart Elden and Gerald Moore. London and New York: Continuum, 2004.
Levine, Caroline. *Forms: Whole, Rhythm, Hierarchy, Network.* Princeton, NJ: Princeton University Press, 2015.
Liszt, Franz. *An Artist's Journey: Lettres d'un bachelier ès musique 1835–1841.* Trans. Charles Suttoni. Chicago, IL: University of Chicago Press, Chicago and London, 1989.
Lloyd, Christopher. *J.-K. Huysmans and the Fin-de-siècle Novel.* Edinburgh, UK: Edinburgh University Press, 1990.
Lyotard, Jean-François. "Sensus Communis." *Le Cahier (Collège Internationale de philosophie)*, no. 3 (March 1987): 67–87.
Mallarmé, Stéphane. *Hérodiade.* Trans. David Lenson. *Massachusetts Review* 30, no. 4 (Winter 1989): 573–88.
———. *Oeuvres Complètes.* Paris: Gallimard, 2003.
Marder, Elissa. "Inhuman Beauty: Baudelaire's Bad Sex." *differences* 27, no. 1 (2016): 1–24.
Marks, Lawrence E. *The Unity of the Senses: Interrelations among the Modalities.* New York: Academic Press, 1978.
McLaughlin, Kevin. *Poetic Force: Poetry after Kant.* Stanford, CA: Stanford University Press, 2014.
Meltzer, Françoise. *Salome and the Dance of Writing: Portraits of Mimesis in Literature.* Chicago, IL: University of Chicago Press, 1987.
Merleau-Ponty, Maurice. *Phenomenology of Perception.* Trans. Colin Smith. London and New York: Routledge Classics, 2002.
Meschonnic, Henri. *Critique du Rythme: Anthropologie historique du langage.* Lagrasse, France: Verdier, 1982.

Morin, Marie-Eve. *Jean-Luc Nancy.* Cambridge, UK: Polity Press, 2012.
Nancy, Jean-Luc. *Being Singular Plural.* Trans. Robert D. Richardson and Anne E. O'Byrne. Stanford, CA: Stanford University Press, 2000.
———. *La Communauté affrontée.* Paris: Galilée, 2001.
———. *La Communauté désavouée.* Paris: Galilée, 2014.
———. *La Communautée désœuvrée.* Paris: Christian Bourgois, 1986.
———. *The Disavowed Community.* Trans. Philip Armstrong. New York: Fordham University Press, 2016.
———. *Être singulier pluriel.* Paris: Galilée, 1996.
———. *The Inoperative Community.* Ed. Peter Connor. Forward Christopher Fynsk. Minneapolis: University of Minnesota Press, 1991.
———. *Listening.* Trans. Charlotte Mandell. New York: Fordham University Press, 2007.
———. *Le partage des voix.* Paris: Editions Galilée, 1982.
———. *Les Muses.* Paris: Galilée (1994) 2001.
———. *The Muses.* Trans. Peggy Kamuf. Stanford, CA: Stanford University Press, 1996.
Nietzsche, Friedrich. *The Birth of Tragedy and The Case of Wagner.* Trans. Walter Kaufmann. New York: Random House, 1967.
———. *Kritische Studienausgabe,* 15 vols. Ed. Giogio Colli and Mazzino Montinari. Munich, Germany: Deutscher Taschenbuch Verlag, 1988.
———. *Untimely Meditations.* Trans. R. J. Hollingdale. Cambridge, UK: Cambridge University Press, 1983.
Nordau, Max. *Degeneration.* Lincoln: University of Nebraska Press, 1993.
Partenie, Catalin, and Tom Rockmore, eds. *Heidegger and Plato: A Dialogue.* Evanston, IL: Northwestern University Press, 2005.
Pasco, Allan H. "'A Rebours' à Rebours." *Revue d'Histoire littéraire de la France.* 109th year, no. 3 (July–September 2009): 621–44.
Payne, Charlton, and Lucas Thorpe. *Kant and the Concept of Community.* Rochester, NY: University of Rochester Press, 2011.
Phillips, Jennifer. "Relative Color: Baudelaire, Chevreul, and the Reconsideration of Critical Methodology." *Nineteenth-Century French Studies* 33, nos. 3/4 (Spring Summer 2005): 342–57.
———. "'Vox populi, vox dei': Baudelaire's Uncommon Use of Commonplace in the Salon de 1846." *French Forum* 31, no. 1 (Winter 2006): 21–39.
Pichois, Claude, and Avice, Jean-Paul. *Dictionnaire Baudelaire.* Charente: Editions du lérot, 2002.
Porter, James I. "Why Are There Nine Muses?" in *Synaesthesia and the Ancient Senses.* Ed. Shane Butler and Alex Purves. Durham, NC: Acumen, 2013.
Ramachandran, V. S., and E. M. Hubbard. "Synaesthesia: A Window into Perception, Thought and Language. *Journal of Consciousness Studies* 8, no. 12 (2001): 3–34.

Rindisbacher, Hans J. *The Smell of Books: A Cultural-Historical Study of Olfactory Perception in Literature*. Ann Arbor: University of Michigan Press, 1992.
Ritter, Joachim, and Gründer, Karlfried. *Historisches Wörterbuch der Philosophie*, vol. 9, Se-Sp. Basel: Schwab, 1971.
Robertson, Lynn C., and Noam Sagiv, eds. *Synesthesia: Perspectives from Cognitive Neuroscience*. Oxford, UK: Oxford University Press, 2005.
Ronell, Avital. *The Test Drive*. Urbana and Chicago: University of Illinois Press, 2005.
Sand, George. *Lettres d'un voyageur*. Paris: Michel Lévy Frères, 1869.
Schlossman, Beryl. "Benjamin's 'Über einige Motive bei Baudelaire': The Secret Architecture of Correspondances." *Modern Language Notes* 107, no. 3 (April 1992): 548–79.
Sng, Zachary. *Middling Romanticism: Reading in the Gaps from Kant to Ashbery*. New York: Fordham University Press, 2020.
Szondi, Peter. *Poésies et Poétiques de la modernité*. Lille: Presses Universitaires de Lille, 1982.
Wagner, Richard. *The Artwork of the Future and Other Works*. Trans. W. Ashton Ellis. Lincoln: University of Nebraska Press, 1993.
———. *Dichtungen und Schriften*. 10 vols. Ed. Dieter Borchmeyer. Frankfurt am Main, Germany: Insel Verlag, 1983.
Ward, Jamie, and Jason B. Mattingly. "Synaesthesia: An Overview of Contemporary Findings and Controversies." *Cortex* 42 (2006): 129–36.
Weber, Samuel. *Benjamin's -abilities*. Cambridge, MA: Harvard University Press, 2008.
Wilkinson, Lynn R. *The Dream of an Absolute Language: Emanuel Swedenborg and French Literary Culture*. Albany: State University of New York Press, 1996.
Zhouhuang, Zhengmi. *Der Sensus Communis bei Kant: Zwischen Erkenntnis, Moralität und Schönheit*. Berlin, Germany: De Gruyter, 2016.
Zuber, Devin P. *A Language of Things: Emanuel Swedenborg and the American Environmental Imagination*. Charlottesville and London: University of Virginia Press, 2019.

Index

Abrams, M. H., 29
actor, 64–72
Adorno, Theodor W., 17–23, 74
Aeolian harp, 27, 29–31, 37
aesthetic synaesthesia, 1, 4–5
affinity, 22, 84, 87, 99–100, 107
Agamben, Giorgio, 11–12, 28
agency, 30–31
analogies, 3, 23, 30, 40, 45–46, 57, 84–85
"Anthropomorphism and Trope" (de Man), 107, 119n2
Apollo, 63–64, 68
À Rebours (Huysmans), 73–89
Aristotle, 2, 4, 11–12, 93
Aristotle on the Concept of Shared Life (Brill), 11–12
aroma. *See* senses; smell
"Art and the Arts" (Adorno), 17–19
artist/hero figure, 64–66
arts, 4–5, 13–23, 59–60
  Huysmans's *À Rebours,* 73–89
  and rhythm, 109–110, 113n14
  unity of, 46–47, 51, 60, 113n14
  See also music; painting
assertion or *Aussage,* 93–95
Athenaeum, 9
attunement, 102–104
audience, 62–63, 70–71

bad synaesthesia, 23
Baudelaire, Charles, 14–17, 23, 39–60, 91–107, 116–117n6, 116n4
Baudelaire and Freud (Bersani), 116n6
Bayreuth, 71–72
"Beacon Lights" ("Les Phares") (Baudelaire), 52–55, 58
Being, call or address of, 103–105
being in common, 10
Being of beings (Sein des Seienden), Heidegger, 99–101
Being-with, 9–11
Benjamin, Walter, 18–20, 41–44, 46, 69
Benjamin's -abilities (Weber), 69
Benveniste, Emile, 109
Bersani, Leo, 116–117n6
bouba and kiki experiment, 2–4
Bright Colors Falsely Seen (Dann), 4
Brill, Sara, 11–12

Calhoun, Doyle, 115n1
Caws, Mary Ann, 115n1
Cerisy-La-Salle, 91, 92
Chladni figures, 114n7
collaboration, 83
The Coming Community (Agamben), 11–12
comme, De Man's reading of, 107, 116n6, 117n14

Index

communication *(Mitteilung)*, 15–16, 64–68. *See also* correspondences
community, 9–23, 63–72
composition, 20–21, 87–88
Concerning the Spiritual in Art (Kandinsky), 13
constellation, 19–21, 42
convergence of media, 21–23, 79, 83–84, 101
Cooke, Peter, 77–78, 118n7
correspondances
  between Baudelaire and Heidegger, 91–107
  Baudelaire's *correspondances*, 14–17
  Baudelaire's synaesthesia, 39–60
  Bersani on, 116n6
  and constellation, 20
  De Man on, 116n3
  and Liszt, 27–28
  Phillips on, 117n19
  Schlossman on, 116n3
  vertical and horizontal, 4, 101, 116n6, 120–121n14
  Wilkinson on, 116n4
"Correspondances" (Baudelaire), 45–58, 107, 116–117n6
"The Correspondent Breeze" (Abrams), 29
The Critical Difference (Johnson), 115n1
criticism, 58–59
Critique du rythme (Meschonnic), 109–110
Culler, Jonathan, 17, 43
Cytowic, Richard E., 1–4

Dann, Kevin T., 4
Das Passagen-Werk (Benjamin), 42, 43–44
Degeneration (Nordau), 74–75
Delacroix, Eugène, 52–58
Deleuze, Gilles, 20, 59, 113n14

de Man, Paul, 107, 111n1, 116n3, 116n6, 117n14, 117n15, 119n2
demonic communicability, 61–72
Der Fall Wagner (Nietzsche), 68–69
Derrida, Jacques, 111n1, 113n10
Der Ursprung des Kunstwerkes (The Origin of the Work of Art) (Heidegger), 119–120n8
"Diderot: Paradox and Mimesis" (Lacoue-Labarthe), 70
diegetic boundaries, 75, 80
"Die Sprache" (Heidegger), 105–106
differentiation, 12, 22, 40, 51
dispersion of the senses, 50, 74, 88–89
The Dream of an Absolute Language (Wilkinson), 116n4

Eagleman, David M., 1–4
"The Echo of the Subject" (Lacoue-Labarthe), 106
eco-poetics, 20
ekphrasis, 75
ek-stasis, 11
England, 29–30
Entsprechung, 92–93, 98–106
event of communication ("Mittheilung"), 61–72
existence as spasm, 115n12
Exposition Universelle (Baudelaire), 58
expression, Adorno's notion of, 22

feelings, 99–100
Fourier, Charles, 41, 107
"Fragment d'une Etude Scenique Ancienne d'un poème de Hérodiade." *See* "Hérodiade" (Mallarmé)
France, 88–89, 94
Freud, Sigmund, 75–76, 89. *See also* smell
friendship, 11–12, 28, 36
"Friendship" (Agamben), 11

Index

"Für—die Philologie" (Hamacher), 102

Gazette musicale, 26
genuine synaesthesia, 1–2
Germany, 29–30
Gesamtkunstwerk, 12, 63–64, 68
Gestalt, 62–63
Gordon, Paul, 42, 111n1
Greek language, 95–98
Greek tragedy, 63–64, 68–69
Grigorian, Natasha, 118n7
Grigson, Geoffrey, 114n8

Hagstrum, Jean, 75
hallucination, 89
Hamacher, Werner, 105–106
Hegel, Georg Wilhelm Friedrich, 13–14
Heidegger, Martin, 91–106, 119–120n8, 120n12, 121n16
Heller-Roazen, Daniel, 12–13
Heraclitus (Heidegger), 104–105
"Hérodiade" (Mallarmé), 80–82
heterogeneity, 14–15, 59–60, 76–77, 101
Hoffmann, E. T. A., 30–31, 46, 57
Hoffmann, J. J., 29–30
Holland, Eugene, 116n6
homologein, 97, 98, 101–102, 104–106
Hubbard, E. M., 3
Hugo, Victor, 51, 57
Huysman, Joris-Karl, 73–89, 118n7

identity, 50–51, 66, 69
"Inhuman Beauty" (Marder), 40–41
inner/outer structure, 29, 32, 70
The Inner Touch (Heller-Roazen), 12
intermediality, 20
intertextuality, 43–44, 51, 107
Ion (Plato), 66
"'It Isn't a Dance'" (Cooke), 118n7

Jakobson, Roman, 120–121n14
Jena Romanticism, 9–10
Johnson, Barbara, 115n1
Jones, W., 30

Kandinsky, Wassily, 13
Kant, Immanuel, 72, 112n6
Kircher, Athanasius, 29
koine aisthesis, 13
Kosman, Aryeh, 12
Krieger, Murray, 75

La communauté affrontée (Nancy), 10–11
La communauté désouevrée (The Inoperative Community) (Nancy), 9–10, 111–112n1
Lacoue-Labarthe, Phlippe, 9–10, 70–71, 110, 112n1, 117n11, 118n5
language, 2–5, 18–19, 40–41, 46, 52, 61–72, 75–76, 85–87, 94–96, 101–106
A Language of Things (Zuber), 116n4
L'Apparition (Moreau), 75–79
Lavater, Johann Kaspar, 32–36
"Le Soleil" ("The Sun") (Baudelaire), 47–48
Le Toucher, On Touching—Jean-Luc Nancy (Derrida), 113n10
L'être singulier pluriel (Bein Singular Plural) (Nancy), 9–10
Letters from Italy (Shelley), 25–26
Lettres d'un bachelier ès musique (Letters of a bachelor of music) (Liszt), 26–27
"L'Heauton timoroumenos" (Baudelaire), 50–51
"L'Invitation au Voyage" (Baudelaire), 39
Liszt, Franz, 26–28, 31–32, 36–37
The Literary Absolute (Lacoue-Labarthe and Nancy), 9–10

The Logic of Sensation (Deleuze), 58, 113n14
Lyotard, Jean-François, 112n6

Mallarmé, Stéphane, 80–83
Marder, Elissa, 40–41
materiality, 13–14, 18–19, 25, 28, 31–32
  of language, 46, 101–102
McLaughlin, Kevin, 44
medium of synaesthesia, 31, 42–43, 57. *See also* rhythm
Meltzer, Françoise, 75–81, 119n8
Merleau-Ponty, Maurice, 14, 21, 113n9
Meschonnic, Henri, 109–110
metaphor, 2–4, 33–34, 55–56, 111n1, 120n14
metonymy, 74, 81, 116n6, 120n14
Middling Romanticism (Sng), 42
Mieszkowski, Jan, 112n6
mimesis, 3, 61, 68–72, 110
mimicry, 2–4
Mitteilbarkeit, 69–72
modernity, 41
Moreau, Gustave, 75–82, 118n7
multiplicity, 17, 23, 109
Les Muses (Nancy), 13, 74
music, 21–23, 25–37, 44–45, 55–59, 62–72, 87–89, 110, 114n7
Musica Ficta (Lacoue-Labarthe), 118n5
mysticism, 20, 39–41, 73–74, 91, 121n14

Nancy, Jean-Luc
  heterogeneity of elements, 59
  Les Muses, 74
  and music, 110
  resonance and dislocation, 46
  rhythm of synaesthesia, 20–23
  sublation of art, 14, 74
  synaesthesia and community, 9–17
  touch for, 113n10
  and Wagner, 66
nature, 14, 29–30, 37, 46–47, 67–72
neurological synaesthesia, 1–2, 4
Nichomachean Ethics (Aristotle), 4, 11–12
Nietzsche, Friedrich, 61–72, 118n5
Nordau, Max, 74–76

"Obsession" (Baudelaire), 53, 117n17
"On Color" (Baudelaire), 55–57
ordinary synaesthesia, 14–15, 21
original phrase, 89
Origin of German Tragic Drama (Benjamin), 19

painting, 21–23, 25–26, 28, 44–45, 58–59, 75–89, 118n7
personification, 64
Phenomenology of Perception (Merleau-Ponty), 113n9
Phillips, Jennifer, 117nn19–20, 118n7
philosophy of correspondence, Heidegger, 91–106
physiognomy, 32–34
physiological nondifferentation, 74
physiology, 1–5
Pichois, Claude, 120–121n14
Plato, 66, 68, 97, 120n12
"Platons Lehre von der Wahrheit" (Heidegger), 97
plurality, 10, 16–19, 23, 49, 104
poetry, 47–48, 52, 57–59, 87–89, 115n1
presentation *(Darstellung)*, 65–66, 71–72
Priscian, 13
prose poem, 39, 82, 85–86
prosopopeia, 35, 75, 80, 83
proto-language, 3
proto-synaesthesia, 3
pseudo-synaesthesia, 1–2

question and answer, 95–97

Ramachandran, V. S., 3
Raphael, 25–26, 28, 32–33
reading, synaesthetic, 25–37
representation, 68, 75, 92–98
resonance, 20, 28–29, 43, 46–47, 50–51, 103–104, 110
rhythm, 17, 20–23, 59, 88, 104, 105, 109–110, 113n14
"Richard Wagner and Tannhäuser in Paris" (Baudelaire), 44–45
Richter, Gerhard, 121n16
Romanticism, 29, 40
Ronell, Avital, 61, 115n12

Salome Dancing before Herod (Moreau), 75–86, 118n7
Salon de 1846 (Baudelaire), 46, 55, 57–58, 117n20
sameness/difference, 103–104
Sand, George, 27–28, 31–37
Schlossman, Beryl, 116n3
Sein und Zeit (Heidegger), 92–93, 96
self, 9, 11–13, 29–31, 48–51, 54, 110
self-alienation, 65–68
self-consciousness, 4
self-differentiation, 15
senses
   Aeolian harp, 30–32
   and the arts, 74–76, 82, 86–89
   in Baudelaire, 45–47, 50–52, 57–60
   and community, 12–23
   and language, 105
   and *Mitteilbarkeit*, 72
   normal perception as a kind of synaesthesia, 113n9
   and perception, 2–5
   and rhythm, 109–110, 113n14
   of synaesthesia, 45–47, 120–121n14
   touch for Nancy, 113n10

unification of, 23, 41–43
   in Wagner, 63
sensus communis, 112n6
"Sept leçons sur *Hérodiade*" (Szondi), 83–84
Shelley, Percy Bysshe, 25–26
singular/singularities, 9–13, 17–19, 43, 46, 49, 52, 57–60, 68
smell, 47, 75–76, 79, 86–89. See also senses
Sng, Zachary, 42
Spiegel, 104
Spielereien, 23
spiritual, 13, 17, 20
spiritual correspondence, 39
St. Cecilia, 25–26, 28, 32–34
sublation of art, 14, 17, 20, 73–74, 78
Swedenborg, Immanuel, 20, 27, 41, 116n4
symbolism, 3–4, 28, 46–47, 56, 78, 82, 84–86, 116n6, 118n7
sympathetic partitioning communication, 67
synaesthesia, 1–5
   in artistic creation, 85–89
   and Baudelaire, 39–60
   and correspondences, 27–28
   and demonic communicability, 63–72
   and language, 105
   normal perception, 113n9
   and rhythm, 17–18, 20–23, 59, 109–110
   and the self, 31
   unworking of in Huysmans's *À Rebours*, 73–89
   vertical and horizontal, 116n6, 120–121n14
   See also convergence of media
"Synaesthesia—A Window into Perception, Thought and Language" (Ramachandran and Hubbard), 3

Synaesthetics (Gordon), 111n1
syncretism, 77
Szondi, Peter, 83–84

The Test Drive (Ronell), 61
thauma, 102
Thomas of Aquinas, 93
touch, 14–17, 59–60, 113n10
"Tout Entière" (Baudelaire), 49–50
transimmanence, 16, 23
translation, 18, 44–46, 63, 91–92, 96–98, 101–102
truth as correspondence, 91–95, 120n12

uncanny, 31
unity, 4–5, 13–15, 19–20, 49–51
  Aeolian harp, 29
  of the arts, 46–47, 51, 60, 113n14
  and Baudelaire's *correspondances*, 40–42
  and communication, 63–64
  and correspondence, 103–104, 107
  of logos and truth in Heraklitis, 96
  and rhythm, 59, 109, 110, 113n14
  of the senses, 23
  and sublation, 74
  See also community
universal symbolism of language, 3–4

Untimely Meditations (Nietzsche), 61–62, 66–67
Unverborgenheit, 92, 96–98
utopian element of the arts, 18

Valéry, Paul, 46, 110
vertical and horizontal, 16–17, 23, 41–42, 101, 116n6, 120–121n14
vision, 2, 25–37, 76, 79
visual, 2–3
"Vom Wesen der Wahrheit" (Heidegger), 94–95

Wagner, Richard, 44–45, 61–72, 73–74, 118n5
"Was ist das—die Philosophie?" (Heidegger), 91–106
Weber, Carl Maria von, 39, 55, 58
Weber, Samuel, 69
Western philosophical tradition, 93
"White Mythology" (Derrida), 111n1
"Why Are There Several Arts and Not Just One?" (Nancy), 13
Wilkinson, Lynn R., 116n4
wisdom, 96–97
Wortmystik, 96

Zhouhuang, Zhengi, 112n6
Zuber, Devin P., 116n4
Zur Sache des Denkens (Heidegger), 120n12

www.ingramcontent.com/pod-product-compliance
Lightning Source LLC
Chambersburg PA
CBHW031403230426
43670CB00006B/628